LOBBYING: INTERACTION AND INFLUENCE IN AMERICAN STATE LEGISLATURES

NEW FRONTIERS IN AMERICAN POLITICS SERIES

Harmon Zeigler, General Editor
University of Oregon

CONGRESS IN CRISIS: POLITICS AND CONGRESSIONAL
REFORM
Roger H. Davidson (University of California, Santa Barbara)
David M. Kovenock (University of North Carolina)
Michael K. O'Leary (Syracuse University)

REFORM AND REACTION: CITY POLITICS IN TOLEDO
Jean L. Stinchcombe (University of Michigan)

LOBBYING: INTERACTION AND INFLUENCE IN AMERI-
CAN STATE LEGISLATURES
Harmon Zeigler (University of Oregon)
Michael A. Baer (University of Kentucky)

FORTHCOMING VOLUMES:

AN AMERICAN POLITICAL DILEMMA: COMMUNITY EDU-
CATIONAL POLITICS
Robert E. Agger (University of Oregon)
Marshall N. Goldstein (University of Hawaii)

BUREAUCRATIC COMMUNICATIONS
Benjamin Walter (Vanderbilt University)

Wadsworth Publishing Company, Inc., Belmont, California

LOBBYING:
INTERACTION
AND
INFLUENCE
IN AMERICAN
STATE
LEGISLATURES

HARMON ZEIGLER
University of Oregon

MICHAEL A. BAER
University of Kentucky

Wadsworth Publishing Company, Inc., Belmont, California

NEW FRONTIERS IN AMERICAN POLITICS SERIES

Political science is a changing discipline, but the changes that are taking place are not very different from those that took place in other social sciences a good many years ago. Briefly, political scientists are becoming interested in empirical (some would say "causal") theory and are seeking the appropriate methodologies that will enable them to develop reliable descriptions of recurring patterns in political life. The nature of the articles that are published in professional journals and monographs, which are no longer the exclusive property of university presses, attest to the general improvement of the discipline. Scholars are beginning to be a little self-conscious about using the term "behavior" as though it designated a specific and unique "branch" of political science.

Graduate education in political science is reflective of this trend. Most departments of political science require that their students acquire a level of sophistication in statistics and research design that would have been considered extreme as late as ten years ago. Thus, a majority of graduate students, rather than a minority as was formerly the case, begin their teaching careers with an appreciation for the importance of a systematic study of political life.

However, one must question the extent to which undergraduate students are exposed to political science research— as it is being conducted today. After all, very few undergraduate students, even if they are political science majors, go to graduate school; and the proportion of political science students who are aware of new developments in research technique or new explorations of "old" substantive areas is probably unfortunately small. Although each year sees the appearance of more texts that rely heavily upon recently published material, one frequently hears the argument that much of the current research is over the heads of undergraduates and must be distilled and compressed to be useful.

It is the assumption of this series that a fruitful way to introduce students to political science research is to let them read it for themselves. They can see the problem faced by the researcher, judge the validity or logic of the methods, evaluate the extent to which evidence is supportive of the conclusions, and formulate some idea of the nature of social research. There is no reason why the pedagogical assumptions of undergraduate instruction should differ from those of the graduate program. If there are facts of political and social life worth knowing, all students should be made aware of them.

Harmon Zeigler
Series Editor

University of Oregon

CONTENTS

TABLES

FOREWORD

HEINZ EULAU

An invitation to write a foreword may be flattering, but it is by no means an enviable assignment. Both the cost and the risk involved are high. In accepting the invitation one surely surrenders that freedom which is the critic's inalienable right. One ought to pay the cost and take the risk only if there are good and substantial reasons for doing so. My justification is necessarily the merits of what I may say in these few paragraphs.

Sometimes, if rarely, one encounters a book which gives one the uncomfortable feeling that one should have written it oneself. The fact that one has not written it in turn gives the book an aura of importance that is perhaps not warranted. Many years ago, a bright and honest student of mine, writing a review, gave a book high praise. "This book," she wrote, "is a good book. This is because it agrees with me. Amazingly, the author is saying things that I have been thinking all along." Of course, thinking that one could have done the book oneself is not enough, for the burden of proof is in the doing and not in the thinking. Yet, what makes a book loom large in one's perspective is just this sense of subjective identification with the author.

All this would be merely banal if it were that a book is fortuitous. In the case of a scientific book we can assume that it is neither banal nor fortuitous. And it is not simply accidental that I find this book exciting. For the authors did not stumble accidentally across some novel ideas or a novel approach to an old subject. Rather, in doing the research that went into this book, they were the descendants of those who have traveled the long road toward a serious and not whimsical science of politics.

The road was opened up in the first decade as a narrow, one-way track by pioneer Arthur F. Bentley. It was traveled on in the twenties and thirties by such eminent political scientists as Peter Odegard and E. Pendleton Herring. In the early fifties it was widened, improved and made fit for modern usage by David B. Truman. But it remained a one-way road. When, somewhat later, John C. Wahlke moved along it, he had a vision of the encounter that a two-way passage might engender. But only now, for the first time, have political scientists ventured to open the road to two-way traffic. This, it seems to me, is the achievement of Professors Zeigler and Baer.

Metaphor aside, there are two things that I find fascinating about this book. First, that the dialectic of the scientific-empirical mode of thinking about politics need not be the kind of vicious argumentation that is the dialectic of sophistry. The book shows that by taking off from what went before, by being critical without being destructive, it is possible to advance theoretical and empirical knowledge about politics in such a way that a cumulative political science becomes possible.

And second, the book shows that a cumulative political science need not be a closed system of thought, but that by introducing relevant interdisciplinary orientations the frontiers of a discipline can be expanded beyond its conventional limits. By bringing the social-psychological theory of interaction to bear on the relationship between legislator and lobbyist, Professors Zeigler and Baer have made a contribution not only to political science but to the behavioral sciences generally.

This book, then, not only continues an honorable line of scholarly efforts to understand and explain the complexities of interest-group politics and legislative politics, but it also pioneers a new line of inquiry. By focussing simultaneously on both sides of the legislator-lobbyist relationship and demonstrating the varieties of contingency defining the relationship, the book represents a new departure in an old field of political investigation. That my own relationship with the senior author has been one of mutual scholarly respect may not be irrelevant in assessing this assessment.

H. E.

Stanford University

PREFACE

The comparative study of state politics has developed along two separate paths. One tradition, with Wahlke, Eulau, Buchanan, and Ferguson's *The Legislative System* as its model, has concentrated upon the attitudes and behaviors of political elites. The other, typified by the work of Thomas R. Dye and Richard Hofferbert, has ignored human behavior in seeking to explain the correlates of policy outcomes. The main thrust of the policy output studies is that politics—measured in terms of party competition, equity of apportionment, and the like—is less crucial than economic development in affecting the amount of money a state will spend. Interpretations of the policy studies—far more simplistic than the work of the original authors—have implied that the process of converting inputs into outputs is less important than the nature of the inputs.

Such interpretations would place the adherents of the two traditions into warring camps. Why study elites? All that is necessary to understand politics is to measure a state's economic potential. Of course, explanations in the social sciences are rarely so simple. The independent variables used by Dye, for example, explain about one third of the variance in the dependent variables. Further, Dye's dependent variables are typically measures of the level of economic support for a given program. Any policy not measurable in financial terms is excluded. The level of measurement for political variables is equally crude. Interest groups are ignored because there is no reliable measure of their strength. Had there been such a measure, it would have been used; such is the level of theory in comparative state politics.

xix

It seems clear that the separate paths of the two traditions are due more to problems of measurement than to problems of theory. We need to seek new measurement techniques in order to test some possible linkages between socioeconomic characteristics, elite behavior, and system outputs. Hofferbert has suggested that elites can serve as mediators between system characteristics and policy outputs. They can serve as activators (thus strengthening the correlation), repressors (weakening the correlation), or—the most difficult role of all—initiators (acting in spite of a predicted economic-policy association).

Measuring elite behavior is more difficult than describing aggregate characteristics. The problem is especially acute when interest groups and lobbyists are the focus of research. Legislatures can be measured by means of roll-call votes, but the only assessment of interest-group strength is derived from asking someone. The necessity of using the interview in studying interest groups introduces the necessity of a choice between alternative strategies of research. On the one hand, one could rely upon a relatively shallow investigation of many states, allowing generalizations about systems but neglecting individual interactions. On the other hand, one can undertake a relatively exhaustive exploration of a few political systems, incurring the liability of a lack of generalizable findings. Being a study of the relationships between legislators and lobbyists in four states, this book represents a choice of the latter strategy. Whether the decision to explore a few systems in depth was appropriate will depend upon the reader's estimate of the worth of the findings. It is important to understand that the book advances a theory of *individual* behavior, using the interactions between legislators and lobbyists as illustrations of the theory.

In the preparation of this book, the authors have profited from the advice and criticism of many colleagues. The senior author attended two seminars: one, in 1966, dealing with the general topic of the study of comparative state politics: the other, in 1968, dealing with the measurement of policy outputs. Both were held under the auspices of the Inter-University Consortium for Political Research, University of Michigan, with financial support from the National Science Foundation. In addition to the participation in these seminars, we received valuable suggestions from Ronald Hedlund, David Wood, and Samuel Patterson. Professor Patterson read the entire manuscript. A special note of thanks is due to Heinz Eulau, whose assistance in the preparation of the manuscript was invaluable.

The interviewing was conducted under the supervision of Roy Bardsley. Analysis of the data was facilitated by the assistance of Richard Styskal, Karl Johnson, Mike Sullivan, and James Hutter. The manuscript was typed by Deidra Hubbell. Finally, we wish to thank Jon Emerson of Wadsworth for his unusual dedication.

The authors also wish to acknowledge the support of the Center for the Advanced Study of Educational Administration, University of Oregon, during a portion of the time they devoted to the preparation of this manuscript. CASEA is a national research and development center which was established under the Cooperative Research Program of the U.S. Office of Education. The research reported in this manuscript was conducted as part of the research and development program of the center.

Harmon Zeigler
Michael A. Baer

1 LOBBYING AS INTERACTION

Heinz Eulau once asked a question which "realistic" students of American politics might regard as absurd. He asked, "What would politics in America be like without lobbies and lobbyists?"[1] To a generation of political scientists raised on the writings of Bentley and Truman, the question seems at first glance not only absurd but reactionary. Concern with interest groups accompanied the development of "modern" political science. When the behavioral revolution reached a fever pitch in the 1950s, political scientists turned first to those writers who rejected the legalism of the past and attempted to describe the interaction of individuals rather than the structure of institutions. Arthur Bentley clearly stood out as a potential source of inspiration. Anybody who, in 1908, could write that "formal study of the most external characteristics of governing institutions" is worthless and that political scientists must instead get hold of "political institutions, legislatures, courts, executive officers, and get them stated as groups, in terms of groups . . ."[2] appeared as a logical choice for the Marx of the behavioral revolution.

Although most political scientists paid little attention to Bentley, various case studies of "pressure groups in action" did appear, culminating in Truman's summary statement, *The Governmental Process*.[3] There are enough ambiguities

[1] Heinz Eulau, "Lobbyists: The Wasted Profession," *Public Opinion Quarterly*, 28 (Spring 1964), 27.

[2] Arthur Bentley, *The Process of Government* (San Antonio, Texas: Principia Press of Trinity University, 1949), p. 210.

[3] David Truman, *The Governmental Process* (New York: Alfred A. Knopf, 1951).

in various group theories to make a direct application of them virtually impossible, but it does seem clear that they claim for interest groups the status of a "first cause" of public policy. Of course, Truman (who replaced Bentley as the leading group theorist) never suggested that in order to study legislation one need only account for the activities of formal groups; but such an unwarranted inference was made by some readers of *The Governmental Process,* if only because data to support Truman's theories was not easily obtained from sources other than formal organizations.

The Group Basis of Politics

The theory that interest groups are, by definition, powerful has been described pejoratively as "mechanistic," meaning that the theory would make legislators merely passive reactors to pressure. In some extreme cases, perhaps, the theory is mechanistic. Yet the better writers on the subject do not argue that all interest groups are powerful or that legislators make decisions solely as a result of their interactions with lobbyists. However, these group theorists do, if all their writings are summed up, outline a model of the political process roughly along the following lines: Individuals in society have a variety of needs, some of which can be achieved only, or most efficiently, through governmental activity. Most of the values and beliefs of individuals are derived from the groups they have contact with. Some of these groups are determined for an individual by circumstance; others are joined voluntarily. Yet even the voluntary joining of an association occurs as a result of the deeper group affiliations of an individual. Since most of the needs of the individual are related to his group affiliations, the logical method of translating these needs into demands is through the formalization of the group. Of course, all groups do not automatically become formal organizations. Formalization can occur only when, through intense and sustained interaction, individuals have systematized their relationships. The existence of organizations of farmers, druggists, doctors, or automobile workers implies that their shared attitudes make it efficient to be represented by a formal group—an interest group. The interest group, by means of its lobbyists, conveys the needs of its members to governmental decision makers.

Thus, group theorists are suggesting that interest groups are "transmission belts" between individual needs and governmental institutions. Other possible channels of communication, especially political parties, are not considered to be as effective, primarily because they are too heterogeneous to be capable of presenting a cohesive point of view.

Froman has provided a useful summary of the function of interest groups as defined by the group theorists. Interest groups, he says, channel communications to decision makers, help to structure alternative policy choices, act as buffers between the government and the people, help check demands made by others, provide functional representation, compartmentalize access to decision makers, lead to a system of minorities rule, and provide people with an emotional outlet.[4] Of course, such a brief outline hardly does justice to the complexities and modifications of traditional group theory, but it does help us to identify the essence of the theory: Interest groups are powerful because they monopolize access to governmental decision makers.

The difficulty with this theory is that the empirical evidence to which it points for justification is based on studies whose design presumed the validity of the theory. In these studies, the prior assumption that lobbyists are influential led to distortion of the findings to fit the model.

One of the authors can provide personal evidence of the confusion which results from an unquestioning acceptance of the group theorists' model. While preparing a study of small business organizations, he discovered that lobbyists for these organizations described themselves as intimately involved in the affairs of the House and Senate Small Business Committees and of the Small Business Administration. However, members of these committees, their staffs, and the administrators of the Small Business Administration not only did not share this evaluation but in many cases did not know the names of the lobbyists! It seemed the decision makers regarded the interest groups as without either power or legitimacy.[5]

This was, of course, only a single case study of one area of public policy, but its findings seemed to fit with what other researchers were finding out at about the same time. Matthews' interviews with legislators led him to conclude that the effects of lobbying were

---

[4] Lewis A. Froman, Jr., ''Some Effects of Interest Group Strength in State Politics,'' *American Political Science Review*, 60 (December 1966), 954.

[5] Harmon Zeigler, *The Politics of Small Business* (Washington, D.C.: The Public Affairs Press, 1961).

greatly exaggerated.[6] Wahlke, Eulau, Buchanan, and Ferguson, in *The Legislative System*, a comparative study of four state legislatures, found substantial state-by-state variations in the power of interest groups.[7] In other words, the power of interest groups was found to be not as clear-cut as the group theorists suggest.

In general, studies of Congressional decision making did not emphasize the influence of interest groups unless such an emphasis was the *a priori* purpose of the investigation. The research of those not committed to group-theoretical notions led to the conclusion that "it is not likely that the effects of lobbying are as great as lobbyists themselves or journalistic writers seem to believe."[8]

Shortly after the publication of *The Legislative System*, two studies of lobbying in Washington took issue more directly with traditional group theory. Bauer, Pool, and Dexter, echoing an earlier protest by Cohen that the legend of "pressure group potency . . . appears to be accepted and passed on without evidence,"[9] discovered that, with regard to reciprocal trade legislation, interest groups were a relatively minor factor in the ultimate decision. According to these authors, "the groups did not appear to have the raw material of great power. We noted shortages of money, men, information, and time."[10] Although the authors are careful to disclaim any intention to suggest that their particular case is typical, their conclusions certainly strike at the heart of the stereotype of the powerful, active interest group. Milbrath, interviewing a random sample of Washington lobbyists, generally supported the conclusion of Bauer, Pool, and Dexter. Finding that only a small portion of lobbyists (9 per cent) are consulted frequently by legislators, Milbrath reasoned that legislators do not feel dependent on the

---

[6] Donald R. Matthews, *U.S. Senators and Their World* (Chapel Hill, N.C.: University of North Carolina Press, 1960), pp. 195–196.

[7] John C. Wahlke, Heinz Eulau, William Buchanan, and LeRoy C. Ferguson, *The Legislative System* (New York: John Wiley, 1962), pp. 311–342. There are some problems in interpreting the data of this study—primarily due to the fact that the sole measure of legislators' relationships with lobbyists is their attitude rather than their actual interaction. These problems will be taken up again.

[8] Harmon Zeigler, *Interest Groups in American Society* (Englewood Cliffs, N.J.: Prentice-Hall, 1964), p. 276.

[9] Bernard C. Cohen, *The Influence of Non-Governmental Groups on Foreign Policy-Making* (Boston: World Peace Federation, 1959), p. 2.

[10] Raymond A. Bauer, Ithiel de Sola Pool, and Lewis A. Dexter, *American Business and Public Policy* (New York: Atherton Press, 1963), p. 398.

information supplied by lobbyists.[11] He used the responses of lobbyists, suggesting that legislators and their staffs do not need them, to argue that the net result of lobbying is minimal.

The Nature of This Exploration

Thus we have come full circle. The group theorists' model has been buried and their notion that interest groups are naturally powerful has been discredited. The argument is now that interest groups (or at least the lobbyists who represent them) could very easily be eliminated from the decision-making process without any appreciable change in public policy. This strikes us as a curious situation. Do we have to decide that the "truth" lies in either one direction or the other? Clearly, we do not. The problem for the researcher is to try to measure the effects of interest groups in different decision-making arenas and to offer some explanations for the variations that exist. This seems to be the thrust of recent arguments by Eulau.

Evaluating Milbrath's study, Eulau agrees that the concept of "pressure" is too "strong" to be useful as an explanatory device for the rationale of lobbying and that "pressure group" is a misnomer. However, he maintains that Milbrath's alternative explanatory model, "communications," is too "weak." By this he means that a definition of the lobbying act as a communications process cannot provide a guide to reliable explanations because the concept is too broad: *Every* social relationship is a communications process. However, correct in his assessment of the nature of communications, Eulau seems to deny Milbrath's communications model its real virtue: its suggestion that interactions between legislators and lobbyists take a variety of forms, with "pressure" being only one, very minor form. That is to say, the concept of communications includes both the notion of pressure and the notion of the transmission of information.

The real virtue of Eulau's criticism is his plea that political scientists should address themselves to "the critical problems of the impact of lobbying on governmental decisions."[12] Apparently, Eulau believes this problem is best approached by means of a model

[11] Lester Milbrath, *The Washington Lobbyists* (Chicago: Rand McNally & Co., 1963).

[12] Eulau, p. 35.

which depends heavily upon a description of the *total* role-defini-
tion system of legislators. In other words, in order to understand
the attitude of legislators toward interest groups (and, by inference, the behavior of legislators with regard to lobbyists), we have
to understand legislators' self-perceptions in relation to their colleagues, constituents, parties, and any other source from which they
derive attitudinal or behavioral cues.

One can hardly quarrel with Eulau's plea, as far as it goes.
However, there are alternative ways of approaching the problem. A
conspicuous gap in *The Legislative System* is the failure of the
authors to pay more than cursory attention to the total environment
in which the legislators perform their functions. This gap is made
even more troublesome by recent research on outputs. Recent efforts
by Dye, Hofferbert, Grumm, and others to explain the outputs of
state legislatures has led to the conclusion that knowing the characteristics of the political system (such as extent of malapportion-
ment, strength of parties, and party cohesion) does not enable one
to predict what kinds of decisions a given state will make.[13] Knowing something about the economic and social environment, on the
other hand, does enable one to make relatively strong predictions
about state outputs. Thus, one can ask the same question of party
organizations that Eulau asked about interest groups: What would
happen if they were to disappear? Clearly, it is not yet possible to
say that nothing would happen, but this kind of question makes
compelling the need to look at total environments. This is not to
assert, however, that environmental conditions *necessarily* influence
the behavior of interest groups; rather, it is to suggest the desirability of *asking* whether or not they do. It may be true that behavioral
patterns, unlike outputs, are not related.

While research on the nationwide level provides an obvious test
of theories concerned with environmental variables, so does research
on the state level. The states, furthermore, are more accessible to
researchers and display as much variety as there is between various
national political cultures. Finally, while there is wide variety
among the socioeconomic environments of the states, there are also
enough institutional similarities to make the task of comparative
research less trying. The research on which this book is based

[13] This literature is evaluated in John G. Grumm, ''Structure and Policy in
the Legislature'' (unpublished manuscript presented at the Conference on the
Comparative Study of State Politics, University of Michigan, August 1–12,
1966).

consists of interviews conducted with legislators and lobbyists in Oregon, North Carolina, Massachusetts, and Utah.[14] These states were selected to provide the study with a maximum dispersion of socioeconomic conditions. (See Chapter 2 for a description of the socioeconomic characteristics of these four states.)

The attention we give to environment is intended not to obscure the importance of individual role perceptions but to provide these perceptions with a setting. Indeed, most of the empirical portions of this paper are based directly upon perceptions of self and perceptions of others. The basic assumption, derived directly from Eulau rather than in opposition to him, is that "one should conduct empirical work . . . at both ends of the legislator-lobbyist relationship."[15] This points to another criticism of *The Legislative System* (derived, as noted, from one of the authors of the book): the reliance of the authors solely on interviews with legislators. It is difficult to draw accurate inferences about the actual nature of the lobbying process without talking to both of the groups involved. When this is not done, the unwarranted assumption is tacitly made that one group or the other is the best judge of what is actually happening. Lockard and Garceau and Silverman indicate that in some cases legislators are actually *not* aware of the "real" world.[16] Lobbyists are not necessarily any more reliable. The inability of either set of participants to provide an "accurate" assessment of the situation is not a function of dishonesty but is simply an illustration of the fact that two actors participating in the same situation may have entirely different perceptions of it. This is true

[14] Interviews were conducted during February and March, 1966. Efforts were made to interview every legislator and lobbyist in all four states. For the legislators, the percentage of completed interviews is Massachusetts, 87%, North Carolina, 97%, Oregon, 94%, and Utah, 94%. For lobbyists, the percentage interviewed is more difficult to assess. In Utah, there is no list of registered lobbyists and in the other states it was found that some lobbyists do not register. In Massachusetts and North Carolina, the number of completed interviews exceeds the number of registered lobbyists. In Oregon, 94% of the registered lobbyists were interviewed. In Utah, since we first had to construct a list based upon preliminary interviews with experienced legislators, newspaper reporters, and the more visible lobbyists, no percentage calculation can be given.

[15] Heinz Eulau and Katherine Hinckley, "Legislative Institutions and Processes," in James A. Robinson, ed., *Political Science Annual* (Indianapolis and New York: Bobbs-Merrill Co., 1966), p. 147.

[16] Duane Lockard, *New England State Politics* (Princeton, N.J.: Princeton University Press, 1959), p. 42; Oliver Garceau and Corinne Silverman, "A Pressure Group and the Pressured: A Case Report," *American Political Science Review*, 43 (September 1954), 672–691.

because "the interpersonal behavior event . . . may be thought of
as a process . . . in which the action of one person is a response to
the second person . . . [and] the actions of each are in reference to
the other."[17] Hence, the role definitions of lobbyists and legislators
are derived as a consequence of their interaction, although neither
lobbyist nor legislator need have shared assumptions about the
purpose of the encounter. (Indeed, some of their behavior might be
a consequence of misperceptions of the purpose of the encounter.)
Note that this model does not imply that the only way to understand the legislator-lobbyist relationship is to account for each
participant's *total* network of interactions and expectations.
Rather, the model implies that the best approach to an understanding of the relationship is through study of the expectations of each
participant with *respect to the other*.[18]

Thus, the research on which this book is based is simply an
analysis of the encounter between legislators and lobbyists within
the context of political culture. The purpose of the research is to
arrive at an assessment rather than a theory. The questions we hope
to answer are (1) how much interaction between legislators and
lobbyists actually takes place? (2) what is the nature of this interaction? and (3) what is the effect of this interaction?

The Nature of Interaction Theory

Theories of interaction have been developed almost exclusively by
social psychologists. Interaction, as they define it, almost invariably
refers to communications between persons. Sometimes these communications are confined to a dyadic situation and sometimes they are
extended to a larger group. Indeed, interaction research and small
group research have developed together and are in many cases
inseparable.

Several refinements must be made in the general view of interaction in order to extract from it an explicit set of hypotheses that can
be empirically tested. A standard definition of interaction serves to

---

[17] David Krech, Richard Crutchfield, and Egerton Ballachey, *Individual in Society* (New York: McGraw-Hill, 1962), p. 4.

[18] On this point, see Edward E. Jones and John W. Thibaut, "Interaction Goals as Bases of Inference in Interpersonal Perception," in Renato Tagiuri and Luigi Petrullo, eds., *Person Perception and Interpersonal Behavior* (Stanford, Calif.: Stanford University Press, 1958).

highlight some of the areas in which refinements must be made. Thibaut and Kelley write:

> By interaction, it is meant that they [two individuals] emit behavior in each other's presence, they create products for each other, or they communicate with each other. In every case we would identify as a case of interaction, there is at least the *possibility* that the actions of each person affect the other.[19]

This definition imposes several restrictions upon the concept of interaction as it applies to legislator-lobbyist relations. First, it is obvious that the interaction must contain an element of *contingency;* that is, the interaction must carry the possibility for the modification of the behavior of one or both of the participants. In Blau's terminology, the possibility for an *exchange* must exist.[20] It is not necessary that a modification of behavior actually occur; it is necessary only that the nature of the interaction or the situation in which it takes place be such that a modification of behavior could occur. It is also not necessary that the contingency of the exchange be asymmetrical. That is to say, for interaction to take place it is not necessary that the flow of influence be entirely in one direction. We do not think of lobbying as a one-way street in which the legislator simply responds to the behavior of the lobbyist without influencing his behavior. Rather, we look on legislator-lobbyist interaction as a reciprocal relationship. Each participant brings into the exchange certain resources, and each participant gives to the other a portion of these resources in exchange for gratifying behavior. The degree of contingency in the interaction will depend in part upon the extent to which either party finds the services (the resources) of the other useful in the achieving of a goal. It may be that the same services can be obtained more economically elsewhere —by means of other interactions. Consequently, the legislator-lobbyist interaction will not necessarily be totally contingent: The behavior of one participant may not be the only influence on the behavior of the other. Indeed, it is likely that several sources of service will compete for the favor of each participant.

A consequence of the definition of interaction outlined above is to give special significance to each actor's perception of the other's

---

[19] John W. Thibaut and Harold H. Kelley, *The Social Psychology of Groups* (New York: John Wiley, 1961), p. 10.

[20] Peter M. Blau, *Exchange and Power in Social Life* (New York: John Wiley, 1964).

motives, values, personality characteristics, and so on. It is very important to each participant in an interaction that he have information about what the other expects to gain from the interaction. In an asymmetrical interaction, such as that which might take place in a military organization or other rigid hierarchy, perceptions of others do not influence behavior to any appreciable extent. In a reciprocal interaction, however, the behavior of each actor is governed largely by his evaluation of the significant other.

To some extent, the evaluation of the other is influenced by the perceived purposes of the interaction. Why do legislators and lobbyists interact? This may seem an absurd question, but the goals of an interaction are more complex than they appear at first glance. Basically, the goals of an interaction can be classified into those concerned with extrinsic rewards and those concerned with intrinsic rewards.[21] The distinction being made here is between interaction as a means to an end and interaction as an end in itself. The actual goals of a particular interaction are usually a mix of these two, and in most cases the goals will change as the interaction continues. The legislator-lobbyist relationship is one devoted primarily to extrinsic rewards. Lobbyists approach legislators and legislators approach lobbyists for extrinsic gratification. This is not to say that intrinsic rewards do not develop out of the relationship, but merely to suggest that the fundamental nature of the association is one in which each participant uses the other to attain a goal beyond that of the interaction itself. In order to make efficient use of the contributions of each other, both participants must work toward gaining a common perception of the shared environment. Toward this end, each attempts to elicit information from the other. Each sizes the other up, estimating the other's potential for influence, his knowledge, and his values. At the same time, each estimates how he appears to the other in terms of these qualities. As the lobbyist sizes up the influence of a legislator, he also forms an evaluation of the legislator's perception of his (the lobbyist's) influence. Interpersonal perception thus becomes a key concept in interaction theory.

A consequence of interpersonal perception, developed by Heider[22] and stated simply in Boulding's "first proposition," is that "be-

[21] Blau, pp. 35–38.

[22] Fritz Heider, *The Psychology of Interpersonal Relations* (New York: John Wiley, 1958).

havior depends on the image."[23] In other words, the course of an interaction depends on the "image" each participant has of the other, the impression each has formed of the other. However, the nature of the image is, in turn, influenced by the course of the interaction. Initially, lacking specific information about a particular partner in interaction, we depend upon stereotypes to develop expectations. In this sense, interpersonal perception theory is analogous to sociological role theory. If we know a person is a white Protestant living in a Midwestern city with a population of 2,000, we expect him to be a Republican and to espouse a conservative political ideology. Arguments directed toward this person are likely to be based upon this expectation, but the expectation may be modified if, during the course of the interaction, certain unique aspects of the person's behavior are uncovered. In the same way, legislators and lobbyists who interact infrequently are likely to base their expectations on stereotypes. However, if the interaction develops into a *relationship* (a repeated set of interactions), stereotypes will be replaced by evaluations based more upon the unique characteristics of a particular lobbyist or legislator than upon perceptions of legislators and lobbyists as a class of persons. Consequently, it is important in using interaction theory to examine frequency of interactions as an independent variable and perceptions of the other as a dependent variable.

Some Problems of Application

A possible problem in the approach adopted in this study is that all of the hypotheses and assumptions of the study are based on experimental small group research, while the empirical findings reported in the study are based upon surveys of larger groups. Hovland and Lipset and his associates have discussed this kind of problem.[24] While it is apparent that the methodologies of experi-

[23] Kenneth E. Boulding, *The Image* (Ann Arbor, Michigan: University of Michigan Press, 1961), p. 6.

[24] Carl I. Hovland, "Reconciling Conflicting Results Derived From Experimental and Survey Studies of Attitude Change," *American Psychologist*, 14 (1959), 8–17; Seymour M. Lipset, Paul F. Lazarsfeld, A. H. Barton, and Juan Linz, "The Psychology of Voting: An Analysis of Political Behavior," in Gardner Lindzey, ed., *Handbook of Social Psychology* (Reading, Massachusetts: Addison-Wesley Publishing Co., 1954), pp. 1124–1175.

mental research differ markedly from those of survey research, the
conclusions of the two methods of research are not likely to differ as
widely as has been assumed in the past. For instance, surveys of the
effects of communications have generally suggested that relatively
few people are affected by communications but that those effects
that do occur are due to personal influence, to personal confrontation rather than to mass communication. Experimental studies, on
the other hand, have begun by concentrating on personal influence
and have recorded significant changes in attitudes. Thus, though
survey research suggests that few attitudes are changed and experimental research suggests that attitude change is widespread, both
agree that personal influence is the key variable in producing a
change. It is this variable that our study was designed to explore.
The extent to which the data reported here can be ordered usefully
according to the hypotheses of small group experimental research is
an empirical question.

The conclusion—led to by both experimental research and survey
research—that personal influence is a more efficient means of producing attitude change than is mass communications raises a challenge to our use of interaction theory in analyzing legislator-lobbyist relationships: To what extent do the responses obtained in our
interviews reflect direct interpersonal exchange as contrasted to
exchange at a level once removed? Exchanges at a level once removed do not contain the element of direct interpersonal perception
which we have defined as crucial to interaction. Thus, it would have
been extremely difficult for Milbrath to have used interaction theory as a tool in his study of Washington lobbyists because he
discovered that those lobbyists tend, out of necessity, to rely heavily
on indirect, nonpersonal communication. Although they believe that
personal contact is a far more effective means of communicating
with a legislator, they seldom have access directly to the legislator.
Most of their communication with legislators is made through staff
members. The size of the national legislative assembly and the relative formality of the national legislative process further hinder the
personal interactions of legislators and lobbyists.[25]

On the state level, however, legislatures are smaller and less
formal and the legislator usually has no staff to act as a buffer.[26] We

[25] See Milbrath, pp. 119–120.

[26] See Harmon Zeigler, ''Interest Groups in the States,'' in Herbert Jacob
and Kenneth N. Vines, eds., *Politics in the American States* (Boston: Little,
Brown and Co., 1965), pp. 101–107.

would therefore expect legislator-lobbyist communication on the state level to be more direct. If this is so, then interaction theory is justified as a way of looking at state lobbying processes, though, at the same time, it loses its ability to generalize beyond the state level. As a test of this hypothesis, we constructed an index which gauged the proportion of his time that a lobbyist devoted to direct face-to-face lobbying as opposed to indirect lobbying through an intermediary or by means of formal communication. We then categorized lobbyists according to which type of communication they used in the majority of cases. As Table 1.1 indicates, only a small proportion of lobbyists in each state relies more heavily upon indirect communication. In all states—even in Massachusetts, with its 280 legislators—direct lobbying is the standard operating procedure. Consequently, we are on relatively safe ground in applying theories of interpersonal perception and behavior to lobbying in the states.

TABLE 1.1

Percentage of Lobbyists (by State) Spending the Majority of Their Time in Three Methods of Communication

	Massachusetts	North Carolina	Oregon	Utah
Direct communication	50%	49%	67%	51%
Indirect communication	12	11	7	15
Both equally	38	36	25	33
Unclassified	1	4	2	2
	101%*	100%	101%*	101%*
(N)	(185)	(132)	(193)	(134)

* Percentages exceed 100 due to rounding.

2 THE ENVIRONMENTAL ARENA

In this study of the process of lobbying, we are especially interested in the dynamics of interaction and the stimulus response elicited from legislators by actions of interest-group representatives. However, as Samuel Patterson has pointed out, a study of the behavior of legislators should take into account the political and social environment in which the legislative system lies.[1] When seeking the explanation for any form of human behavior, one is faced with a multiplicity of causes. In concentrating upon interaction, we are not suggesting that environmental variables are not important; we are suggesting only that they are less immediate to the interaction and hence less capable of being used directly as explanatory factors. In terms of an etiological sequence, we can identify historical, politico-economic, and situational factors as further removed from the act of interaction than, for example, self-perception. However, environmental factors such as these set the stage for interaction. Legislatures were not created yesterday. They have been in business for many years and have developed distinctive styles. Further, the normative and role structures of the legislature will be, to some extent, a microcosmic representation of the broader society. Finally, the formal structure of the legislature, the way it conducts its business, the structure of groups surrounding legislative decision making, and the organization of political parties

[1] Samuel C. Patterson, ''Research on State Legislative Behavior: Notes on Etiological and Comparative Perspectives'' (unpublished paper prepared for Research Conference on Comparative State Politics, University of Michigan, August 1966).

are aspects of the situation which impose constraints upon legislative behavior (whether or not the individual is aware of these constraints). This chapter is devoted to a brief summary of this kind of background information for the states chosen for our study—Massachusetts, North Carolina, Oregon, and Utah.

Environmental Variables

We are aware that each state within the United States bears great resemblances to other states. But, when making a comparative analysis of individual behavior in the states, we must recognize the environmental variations that are also found. Many of these variations will be pointed out in the six sections that follow: (1) socioeconomic variations, (2) tenure and compensation, (3) size of chamber and party balance, (4) party systems, (5) legislative procedures, and (6) interest groups. Though there is no way of causally linking these background variables to the behavior of legislators and lobbyists, we might infer (lacking additional information) that observed differences in behavior among the legislators in different states are related to differences in environments. However, the point will be made later that the effect of environmental variables is randomly distributed with respect to the strength of interest groups. Nevertheless, environment serves as a conditioning factor for the attitudes of both legislators and lobbyists, attitudes which, in turn, regulate the *behavior* of interest groups.

Socioeconomic Variables

Massachusetts, North Carolina, Oregon, and Utah were selected for study to provide a maximum range not only of legislative conditions but also of socioeconomic variations. These four states were not selected as representatives of different regions of the country, and in certain ways they are clearly atypical of the regions in which they lie. For instance, as Key has noted, "the prevailing mood in North Carolina is . . . at odds with much of the rest of the South." The state government of North Carolina has been unmarred by political scandals for more than half a century; the state university is well known for its academic freedom; and though racial attitudes within the state are not perfect, North Carolina does have a reputation for dealing fairly with its Negro citizens.[2] Utah, too, in at least one way, is unrepresentative of the region in which it is located. Whereas about 51 percent of Utah's residents are Mormons, only 4 percent of the citizens of the other Mountain States are Mormons.[3]

In many other ways, however, the four states of our study are representative of the regions in which they lie and differ from each other partly because of these regional biases. For example, Massachusetts, lying in the heavily populated northeastern region of the United States, has a population density of 684 persons per square mile—more than six times the population density of North Carolina, thirty-four times that of Oregon, and fifty-seven times that of Utah (see Table 2.1).

In Massachusetts, 28.8 percent of the population is of foreign parentage, compared to only 1 percent of North Carolina's population. However, almost one quarter of the population of North Carolina is Negro, compared to a very small percentage of the populations of the other three states. North Carolina, typical in this respect of the South, is less urbanized than any of the other three states; its population also has less education and a lower income than the populations of the states of the other regions. Utah, the Mountain State, and Oregon, of the Pacific Northwest, both have smaller populations than our eastern or southern state, but at the same time the populations of both Utah and Oregon are increasing far more rapidly and the mobility of their populations is greater than that of the other two states.

As the large proportion of Mormons in Utah suggests, religion has played an important part in the politics and economics of that state. From 1941 to 1959, the Utah legislature was 89 percent Mormon.[4] It has been estimated that 80 percent of the jobs doled out by the executive branch in Utah have been given to Mormons.[5] Religion is also an important factor in Massachusetts, where the Roman Catholic Church is politically influential, particularly in the

---

[2] V. O. Key, *Southern Politics* (New York: Vintage Books, 1949), pp. 205–206.

[3] National Council of Churches of Christ, *Churches and Church Membership in the United States* (New York, 1956–1958).

[4] Frank H. Jonas, ''Utah: Crossroads of the West,'' in Frank H. Jonas, ed., *Western Politics* (Salt Lake City: University of Utah Press, 1961).

[5] JeDon A. Emenhiser, ''Politics of Utah's Legislature'' (unpublished mimeo, Utah State University).

TABLE 2.1

Socioeconomic Variables in Four States*

	Massachusetts	North Carolina	Oregon	Utah
Total population, July 1, 1966	5,383,000	5,000,000	1,955,000	1,008,000
Percent population increase, 1960–1966	4.7	9.1	10.6	13.1
Percent urban, December 31, 1965	82.1	41.0	62.7	75.4
Population per square mile, 1966	684	102	20	12
Percent Negro	2.2	24.5	1.0	0.5
Percent foreign parentage	28.8	1.0	13.0	12.0
Population mobility: percent of 1960 population residing in different county than 1955 residence	13.5	15.6	25.7	21.2
Percent living in largest SMSA**	49.7	6.7	39.9	45.6
Per capita income, 1965	3,050	2,041	2,761	2,355
Percent failure, Draft Board Mental Tests, 1965	13.0	41.8	7.5	6.8
Median school years completed	11.6	8.9	11.8	12.2
Industrialization index***	98.7	86.7	92.1	94.0

* Sources: *Rankings of the States*, 1967, Research Division, National Education Association, Report 1967-Ri (Washington, D.C., 1967); U.S. Bureau of the Census, *Statistical Abstract of the United States, 1967* (Washington, D.C., 1967).

** Standard Metropolitan Statistical Area.

*** Percentage of population not employed in agriculture, forestry, or fishing.

Democratic Party. From 1945 to 1951, 93 percent of the Democrats in the Massachusetts legislature were Roman Catholics.[6] Since 1900, the majority of the Roman Catholics in the Massachusetts General

[6] V. O. Key, *American State Politics* (New York: Alfred A. Knopf, 1956), pp. 261–262. Key based his information on the 76 percent of the members of the lower House whose religion he could infer from available biographical material.

Court (the legislature) have been of Irish descent, but today an
ever increasing proportion are of Italian heritage.[7]

It has long been established that socioeconomic factors affect
public participation in politics. Well-educated persons with high
incomes, for example, are more likely to vote in a given election
than are poorly educated persons with low incomes. Because of the
differences in the socioeconomic environments of the four states, we
would expect the degree of political activity of their citizens to vary
also. Table 2.2 shows the percentage in each state of the civilian

TABLE 2.2

Election Turnout of Civilian Population

	*1960 Presidential**	*1964 Presidential***	*1952–1960 Gubernatorial and Senatorial, Non-Presidential Years**
Massachusetts	76.1%	72.4%	58.8%
North Carolina	53.5	53.2	25.1
Oregon	72.3	69.7	55.0
Utah	80.1	79.2	64.3
National	63.8	63.0	—

* Lester Milbrath, "Political Participation in the States," in Herbert Jacob and
Kenneth N. Vines, eds., *Politics in the American States* (Boston: Little, Brown and
Co., 1965), pp. 38–40.

** U.S. Bureau of the Census, *Statistical Abstract of the United States, 1967*
(Washington, D.C., 1967), p. 379.

population of voting age that turned out to vote in the 1960 and
1964 Presidential elections and the average percentage that turned
out for the gubernatorial and senatorial elections in non-Presiden-
tial years between 1952 and 1960. As the chart indicates, the states
rank in the same order in all three categories. Every state except
North Carolina ranks above the national average, with Utah consistently having the highest turnout of any of the states. The median
educational levels and the per capita incomes reported in Table 2.1
might have led us to suspect these results.

[7] Duane Lockard, *New England State Politics* (Princeton, N.J.: Princeton
University Press, 1959), p. 134.

Tenure and Compensation

If mean tenure were the only statistic we considered, we would probably conclude that there was no significant difference among the four states of our study in the average experience of legislators. For all but one of those states, the mean length of time a member has served in the legislature is between six and seven years (Table 2.3). Only for Utah is the figure substantially different, the average member there having been in the legislature for only four and one

TABLE 2.3

Legislative Experience

	Average Number of Days Per Year in Session*	Mean Tenure in Years	Index of Experience**
Massachusetts	230	6.6	1,518
North Carolina	66	6.2	409
Oregon	68	6.9	469
Utah	28	4.5	126

* Based on 1961–1966. Source: Council of State Governments, *The Book of the States 1965–1966* (Chicago, 1966).

** The product of average number of days in session multiplied by mean tenure in years.

half years.[8] But, as Wahlke and his colleagues have pointed out, we cannot judge experience by tenure alone, for the amount of time a legislator spends on legislative business per year varies considerably

[8] Curiously, the average age of Utah legislators is much greater than that of legislators in other states. Obviously, since their mean tenure is so low, Utah legislators must enter the legislature late in life. This might be evidence of the unique role the Mormon Church plays in the careers of Utah politicians. In Chapter 3, we note that while about 50 percent of legislators in other states have held other governmental positions prior to entering the legislature, only about half this percentage have held such positions in Utah. On the other hand, most Utah legislators have held prior positions as Mormon bishops (the Mormon religion is disproportionately represented in the legislature). It might therefore be inferred that a Mormon begins a political career only after he has spent some time in service for the church. Hence the late entry of Utah legislators.

from state to state.[9] Whereas the Massachusetts legislature has not been in session for less than 100 days per year since 1860 and averages 230 days in session per year,[10] the Utah legislature meets on the average for only 28 days per year, less time than the legislature of any other state in the union, with the exception of Wyoming.[11] We would expect that members of a legislature which is in session well over half the year would be more experienced legislators than would members of a legislature which is in session less than one month out of the year.

In Table 2.3, we have indicated the mean tenure of members of the legislature in each of the states and the average number of days the legislature has been in session per year from 1961 through 1966. Taking our cue from Wahlke, we have multiplied the mean tenure by the average number of days in session per year and arrived at an index of experience. This index represents the approximate number of days that the average legislator in each of the states has participated in legislative business. Whereas the Massachusetts legislator has an extremely high level of experience, the Utah legislator has an extraordinarily low level of experience. We would expect these levels of experience to play a large role in the atmospheres of the legislatures.

The amount of time a legislator feels he is able to devote to legislative work may also affect the way business is conducted in the legislature. If a legislator received very little financial compensation for his efforts, he would be likely to feel he could not devote much of his time to legislative tasks. If, on the other hand, he received enough compensation to enable him to be free from other jobs (as do members of Congress) he would be able to devote his entire working time to legislative business. Table 2.4 indicates that only in Massachusetts does legislative salary provide the major portion of family income for a large number of legislators. We assumed that if a legislator's family income was equal to or less than his minimum legislative compensation plus one third, then his major source of income was his job as state legislator. By this criterion, 38 percent of Massachusetts legislators receive the major part of their income from the legislature. Less than 5 percent of

[9] John C. Wahlke, Heinz Eulau, William Buchanan, and LeRoy C. Ferguson, *The Legislative System* (New York: John Wiley, 1962), p. 49.

[10] Barry M. Portnoy, ''The Legislative System in the Massachusetts House of Representatives'' (Senior Honors Thesis, Harvard University, 1967), p. 4.

[11] Emenhiser, p. 9.

TABLE 2.4

Legislators' Income

	Minimum Annual Compensation*	Minimum Annual Compensation, Plus One Third	Percentage of Legislators Whose Major Income Source Is State Legislature
Massachusetts	$8,400	$11,200	38%
North Carolina	4,200	5,600	5
Oregon	2,100	2,800	0
Utah	650	867	0

* Source: Council of State Governments, *The Book of the States, 1965-1966* (Chicago, 1966).

North Carolina legislators receive the major part of their income from legislative sources, and none of the legislators do so in Oregon or Utah.

The annual compensation noted in Table 2.4 is based on minimum legislative salary. Many members of the legislature receive additional travel and expense funds due to special sessions, or the distance of their homes from the state capitol, or for service rendered in addition to normal legislative duties. For example, the chairman and vice-chairman of the Massachusetts Ways and Means Committee receive a 50 percent increment above base legislative pay.[12]

Size of Chamber and Party Balance

The size of the legislative chambers of the states we studied ranges from 27 members in the Utah Senate to 240 members in the Massachusetts House (see Table 2.5). The formality and complexity of the rules and procedures governing operations in a legislative chamber will, of course, vary to a great extent with the size of the chamber. In each of the states the Senate is small enough that each member is likely to be well acquainted with each of the other members, and we would expect communication procedures in these chambers to be relatively informal. However, the House of Repre-

[12] Portnoy, p. 77.

sentatives in each state is considerably larger, especially in North
Carolina and Massachusetts. Since the number of possible dyads
within each House or Senate increases geometrically as the size of
the chamber increases numerically, there are 28,680 possible two-
man combinations in the Massachusetts House of Representatives,
but only 351 possible two-man combinations in the Utah Senate.
Obviously there cannot always be communication between each of
the members of a chamber as large as the Massachusetts House. We
would expect, then, that the channels of communication of such a
chamber would be more formalized and that its members would, of
necessity, be influenced to a greater extent by their party.

TABLE 2.5

Number of Members and Party Balance of Each Legislative Chamber

| | Massachusetts | | | North Carolina | | | Oregon | | | Utah | | |
	H	S	G*	H	S	G	H	S	G	H	S	G
Democrat	170	27		106	49	x	32	11		39	15	x
Republican	69	13	x	14	1		28	19	x	30	12	
Total	240**	40		120	50		60	30		69	27	

    * H = House of Representatives
      S = Senate
      G = Governor
    ** 1 Independent

The 1965–1966 session, during which we conducted our interviews with legislators and lobbyists, was typical in terms of party
balance for all four states. In North Carolina, both legislative
houses and the executive branch were controlled, as has been the
case consistently since Reconstruction, by the Democratic party. In
Utah, the Democrats had control of both the legislative and the
executive branches of the government. In the other two states,
however, control was split between the two parties. In Massachusetts, the Democrats controlled both houses in the General Court by
a large margin, but the governor was a Republican. In Oregon, the
governorship and the Senate majority were held by the Republicans, but the Democrats held a slight margin in the House of
Representatives.

Party Systems

We have seen that in the legislative year 1965–1966, the period during which our interviews were conducted, seven of the eight legislative chambers of our study were controlled by Democratic majorities. Three of these states, however, are rated two-party states by the Ranney index of interparty competition.[13] The Ranney index is a computation for the years 1946 through 1963 involving the average percentage of the popular vote going to the Democratic Party in gubernatorial races, the average percentage of Democratic seats in the state Senate and House of Representatives, and the percentage of all gubernatorial, Senate, and House terms in which

TABLE 2.6

Ranney Index of Interparty Competition*

Massachusetts	North Carolina	Oregon	Utah
.5227	.8793	.3545	.4605

* Source: Austin Ranney, "Parties in State Politics," in Herbert Jacob and Kenneth N. Vines, *Politics in the American States* (Boston: Little, Brown and Co., 1965), p. 65.

the Democrats were in control. The Ranney scale ranges from 0.0, which would indicate a solidly Republican state, to 1.0, which would indicate a solidly Democratic state. Table 2.6 shows the rankings on this index of the four states we are studying. Massachusetts and Utah rank very near the middle of the scale and therefore may be considered two-party states with extremely high interparty competition. Even though Oregon's lower score on the index might lead us to think it approaches a modified one-party Republican state, we shall see that this characterization is changing and that in actuality Oregon can currently be considered an extremely solid two-party state. North Carolina, as we might expect of a southern state, ranks very high on the scale, falling in the upper ranges of Ranney's class of "modified one-party Democratic states."

[13] Austin Ranney, "Parties in State Politics," in Herbert Jacob and Kenneth Vines, eds., *Politics in the American States* (Boston: Little, Brown and Co., 1965), p. 64.

Nationally, two-party states tend to have relatively high party cohesion within their legislatures and one-party and modified one-party states tend to have relatively low party cohesion. This generalization holds for Massachusetts—a strong two-party state with strong party cohesion—and, to some extent, for Utah—a strong two-party state with moderate party cohesion—but it does not hold for Oregon or North Carolina.[14] Oregon, a two-party state, has been found to have weak party cohesion. (Thus, our three solid two-party states vary in the party influence that exists within their legislatures.) North Carolina, a modified one-party state, has been found to have strong party cohesion. Key's explanation for this is that the Republican party in North Carolina is strong enough to give politics there the earmarks of a two-party structure even though the party is not strong enough to threaten Democratic supremacy.[15]

In order to gain further insight into party politics in the states of our study, let us look briefly at the historical emergence of the party system in each of these states.

Massachusetts. Though presently the Democrats seem to have a slight advantage in Massachusetts, this has not always been the case. It was a long time before the Democrats obtained any power at all in Massachusetts state politics. It took an influx of large numbers of foreign-born residents and the industrialization of the Northeast to give rise to Democratic victories. In three successive annual gubernatorial elections beginning in 1890, the Democrats did elect a governor of Massachusetts, and, beginning in 1910, they did win five successive gubernatorial races. Even so, however, between 1900 and 1928, the Republicans captured a median of 54.1 percent of the votes for the governorship. The tide turned in 1928 with the presidential candidacy of Al Smith, an Irish Catholic. From 1928 through 1956, the Democrats won eight of fifteen gubernatorial races with a median of 50.3 percent of the votes.[16] The trend in other Massachusetts statewide offices has been the same. While from 1900 to 1911, only 4 percent of the Democrats running for state-

---

[14] For a discussion of party cohesion in these states, see. Belle Zeller, ed., *American State Legislatures* (New York: Thomas Y. Crowell Co., 1954), pp. 190–191.

[15] Key, *Southern Politics*, p. 222.

[16] Lockard, pp. 122–124.

wide offices were elected, from 1942 to 1952, 54 percent of those running were elected.[17]

North Carolina. The Republican party in North Carolina has never been able to make a serious bid for the governorship, and, recognizing that victory on the statewide level is impossible, the party leadership has focused Republican efforts on local and district offices in areas where high concentrations of Republican voters give the party a chance for victory. These efforts have been somewhat successful. By concentrating on local offices, the Republicans have influenced the Democratic party considerably; in fact, because the Republicans are strong in certain areas, North Carolina is one of the few southern states with a formal and strongly cohesive Democratic party organization.

Republican strength comes mainly from the western regions of the state, from the counties which historically had the fewest slaves and the least arable land.[18] In fact, of the fifteen Republican members of the state legislature in the 1965–1966 session, thirteen were elected from counties in the western half of the state.

Oregon. Oregon has always been known as an independent-minded state. Though the Republicans generally dominated state politics until after World War II, the Democrats sometimes took advantage of divisions in Republican ranks caused by third-party movements to elect an occasional governor or senator.[19] Since the Depression, Republican registration in Oregon has dropped steadily, until, in 1954, the majority of the state's voters were registered as Democrats. This trend has provided the Democrats with at least their share of political offices. Indeed, although the Republicans had until shortly before overwhelmingly controlled both houses of the state legislature, in 1958, for the first time in eighty years, and again in 1960 and 1962, the Democrats were able to win control of both houses. Since 1964, however, the state legislature has been split in party control.

Utah. Utah has been solidly bipartisan since it became a state in 1896. Between 1928 and 1966, for example, the Utah House was

[17] Key, *American State Politics*, pp. 155–156.

[18] Key, *Southern Politics*, pp. 218–228.

[19] John M. Swarthout, ''Oregon: Political Experiment Station,'' in Frank H. Jonas, ed., *Western Politics* (Salt Lake City: University of Utah Press, 1961), pp. 262–267.

controlled eight times by the Republicans and eleven times by the Democrats; the Senate was controlled eight times by the Republicans and twelve times by the Democrats. Only between the mid-1930s and the mid-1940s did a large Democratic majority consistently prevail in the Utah legislature; otherwise, control has shifted from year to year. The balance of the parties is indicated by the percentage of the vote which went to the Democratic candidate for governor in the period 1912 to 1952. The Democrats obtained a mean majority vote of only 50.9 percent in this forty-year period.

Prior to the 1965 session of the state legislature, a three-man federal district court ordered a reapportionment of the Utah legislature. Incredibly, a Democratic legislature, operating with a Democratic executive branch, proceeded to reapportion itself in such a way that in the election of 1966, the majority in the Senate was reversed, with only 5 Democrats but 23 Republicans winning seats. The Democratic majority in the House also became a minority, with only 9 Democrats, as opposed to 60 Republicans, winning seats.[20] The respondents in our study were the members of the legislature which reapportioned itself to give to the Republicans the largest majority they had ever had in the history of Utah.

Legislative Procedures

Although the legislatures of all four states of our sample are organized along the general lines of the federal Congress, we do find among them some basic differences in legislative procedures. The most unusual procedure is followed by the Massachusetts General Court, which has a system of "free petition" under which any citizen may present a bill to the legislature simply by obtaining the countersignature of any member of the General Court. Rarely does even a legislator who opposes a particular free-petition bill refuse to put his signature to it.[21] This may account for the exceptionally high number of bills introduced to the Massachusetts legislature and for the exceptionally low proportion of bills introduced to it that are enacted by that legislature (see Table 2.7).

Because of the limited time most state legislatures meet, they generally set time limits beyond which no bill may be introduced.

[20] Emenhiser, pp. 16–33.
[21] Lockard, p. 149.

TABLE 2.7

Bills in the State Legislatures, 1965*

	Number of Bills Introduced	Number of Bills Enacted	Proportion of Introduced Bills Enacted
Massachusetts	5,755	1,048	.18
North Carolina	1,804	1,302	.72
Oregon	1,387	633	.46
Utah	508	197	.39

* Source: Council of State Governments, *The Book of the States, 1965–1966* (Chicago, 1966).

Oddly enough, however, the legislature with the strictest time limit is the only full-time legislature—the Massachusetts legislature. To introduce a bill to the Massachusetts legislature, one must present it one month before the session begins. In the other three states, the limit is set at some point during the session, usually about one month after the session begins. In North Carolina, in fact, though a bill-drafting service[22] is available continuously throughout the year, pre-session filing of bills is not even allowed. Table 2.8 indicates the variations that exist among the four states in the aid available

TABLE 2.8

Procedural Rules on Bills*

	Time Limit on Introduction	Pre-session Drafting Service Available	Pre-session Filing Allowed	Committees Required to Report Bills
Massachusetts	One month before session	Yes	Required	Yes
North Carolina	Fixed at session	Yes	No	Yes
Oregon	35th day	Yes	Yes	No
Utah	Senate–30th day House–35th day	No	Yes	Yes

* Source: Council of State Governments, *The Book of the States, 1965–1966* (Chicago, 1966).

[22] Because of the esoteric nature of legal language, most legislative bodies provide a staff to aid legislators in properly wording the bills they wish to introduce.

in drafting a bill, the limitations on filing a bill, and the responsibility of committees in reporting a bill.

Another unique procedural aspect of the Massachusetts legislature is its system of joint committees. This may be very important to the lobbyist, as it enables him to avoid having to repeat testimony, once to a House committee and again to a Senate committee. As Table 2.9 indicates, the Massachusetts House and Senate have relatively few individual standing committees but have 31 joint committees, precisely 30 more than each of the other three states.[23]

TABLE 2.9

Number of Standing Committees*

	House	Senate	Joint
Massachusetts	6	4	31
North Carolina	46	34	1
Oregon	16	20	1
Utah	16	14	1

* Source: Council of State Governments, *The Book of the States, 1965–1966* (Chicago, 1966).

Interest Groups

Each of the state legislatures is attended by at least as many lobbyists as there are legislators. Though the goals of lobbyists appear to be similar from state to state, all four states do not have the same kinds of laws governing the activities of lobbyists. For instance, only in Massachusetts and North Carolina are lobbyists required to register or to report their expenditures (see Table 2.10). In Oregon and Utah the law governing lobbying states only that "improper activities" (left completely undefined) are prohibited to lobbyists. The penalties for noncompliance with lobbying laws also vary from state to state and to a certain extent reflect the subjective feelings of the legislators in each state. In Utah, for example, where legislators are more hostile toward lobbyists (an attitude recognized by lobbyists, who prefer to be known as "legislative counselors"[24]), the penalty for improper activities is a fine of from $500 to $10,000, or five years imprisonment, or both. This penalty is $8,000 larger

[23] Lockard, p. 149.
[24] Jonas, p. 296.

and three years longer than the next most severe sanction in our sample (and $5,000 larger than in any other state in the Union).[25] Massachusetts law also reveals a subjective judgment on the part of the legislators. The penalty for breaking the lobbying laws in that state can include disbarment, indicating a perception by legislators that many lobbyists are lawyers.

More important to a study of the behavior of lobbyists than knowledge of the legal aspects of lobbying is knowledge of which interest groups are represented and the strength of these interest

TABLE 2.10

Lobbying Regulations and Penalties*

	Registration Required	Expenditures Report Required	Improper Activities Prohibited	Penalties
Massachusetts	Yes	Yes	—	$100–1,000; disbarment
North Carolina	Yes	Yes	—	$50–2,000; 2 years
Oregon	—	—	Yes	$50–500; 1 year
Utah	—	—	Yes	$500–10,000; 5 years

* Source: Legislative Study Committee of the Utah Legislative Council, *Final Report* (Salt Lake City, 1966), p. 129.

groups in each of the states. Many of the same groups are among the most heavily represented in all four states. In each state, we ascertained the ten organizations that had the most lobbyists representing them. Table 2.11 shows which types of organizations rank among the ten most heavily represented in one or more states. Four types were among the most heavily represented in all four states and another five were among the most heavily represented in at least three of the states. Six more groups were heavily represented, but only in one or two states. In Oregon, for example, where timber is the major industry, the lumber and timber lobby was heavily represented. In Utah, where the land is sparsely populated, the conservationists had one of the ten largest lobbying groups.

But knowing only the number of lobbyists representing an interest group does not allow us to make an accurate estimate of the

[25] Legislative Study Committee of the Utah Legislative Council, *Final Report* (Salt Lake City, 1966), p. 129.

TABLE 2.11

Interest Groups Heavily Represented in the Sample States

4 States	3 States	2 States	1 State
Single Business or Corporation	Labor Unions (1, 3, 4)*	Financial, Banks (2, 3)	Lumber, Timber (3)
Trade or Business Association	Insurance (1, 2, 3)	Railroads (2, 3)	Conservationists (4)
Welfare or Public Health	Agriculture (2, 3, 4)	Civil Liberties (1, 4)	Civic Groups (1)
Professional	Governmental Units (1, 2, 4) Education (1, 2, 4)		

*1 = Massachusetts
2 = North Carolina
3 = Oregon
4 = Utah

strength of the group. The most powerful interest group in a state may employ only one or two lobbyists, while a weak group may be represented by many highly active amateur lobbyists. Consequently, some standard other than numbers must be used to ascertain the strength of an interest group. Theoretically, observations of interaction between legislators and lobbyists might be used to judge which interest groups are most influential. It is impossible, however, to observe every interaction between every legislator and every lobbyist, and, even if this could be done, one would still have little or no basis for a judgment of the kind or degree of influence the interaction had had upon the legislator. For this study, we chose a more practical method of measuring strength. We decided to ask a panel of knowledgeable judges to rate the interest groups in terms of power. We considered the participants themselves, the legislators and the lobbyists, to constitute the most knowledgeable panel available. We therefore asked legislators and lobbyists separately to identify the most ''powerful'' groups in their states. We then ranked those groups for each state by the number of times they were mentioned by legislators and the number of times by lobbyists (Table 2.12). Admittedly, use of an emotionally charged word like ''powerful'' and reliance upon the personal judgments of two ''panels'' of men are not likely to produce more than an estimate of the actual influence of an interest group. However, reasonably consistent agreement between legislators and lobbyists on the degree of powerfulness of particular interest groups would indicate a valid assessment of the relative power of various interest groups. Table 2.12 demonstrates a significant degree of consistent agreement.

In many cases the same groups are powerful in more than one state. In all four states, for example, education ranks among the four most powerful groups as rated by both legislators and lobbyists. Labor ranks as powerful in every state but North Carolina, where the labor movement is not yet as established as in non-southern states. In other cases, certain states harbor unique groups related to that state's own industries. In North Carolina, trucking is one of the major industries and the trucking lobby is considered to be the most powerful interest group by lobbyists and the third most powerful group by legislators. In Massachusetts, where many of the large insurance companies have their home offices, the insurance lobby is rated as the second most powerful lobby in the state by both legislators and lobbyists. Another interest group unique to Massachusetts is that of the horse-racing industry, which, though

TABLE 2.12

The Ten Most Powerful Organizations, as Ranked by Each Panel of Judges for Their Own State

MASSACHUSETTS		NORTH CAROLINA		OREGON		UTAH	
Legislators	Lobbyists	Legislators	Lobbyists	Legislators	Lobbyists	Legislators	Lobbyists
Labor	Labor	Electricity (Public)	Trucking	Labor	Labor	Education	Education
Insurance	Insurance	Education	Education	Education	Education	Labor	Labor
Education	Trade and Business Associations	Trucking	Governmental Units	Agriculture	Agriculture	Governmental Units	Trade and Business Associations
Financial, Banks	Education	Electricity (Private)	Agriculture	Trade and Business Associations	Insurance	Agriculture	Agriculture
Trade and Business Associations	Civil Liberties	Utilities*	Labor and Public Employees (tie)	Governmental Units	Trade and Business Associations	Mining	Mining

| MASSACHUSETTS | | NORTH CAROLINA | | OREGON | | UTAH | |
Legislators	Lobbyists	Legislators	Lobbyists	Legislators	Lobbyists	Legislators	Lobbyists
Utilities*	Financial, Banks	Railroads	Electricity (Public)	Electricity (Private)	Utilities*	Trade and Business Associations	Governmental Units
Racing	Utilities*	Governmental Units	Single Business	Insurance	Lumber	Single Business or Corporation	Professional
Single Business	Single Business	Agriculture	Beer, Liquor	Electricity (Public) and Utilities* (tie)	Governmental Units	Electricity (Public)	Single Business
Electricity (Public)	Professional	Insurance	Financial, Banks	Railroads	Professional	Utilities*	Religions
Civil Liberties	Racing	Public Employees			Railroads	Professional and Public Employees (tie)	Civil Liberties

* Not electricity.

not large, has acquired a good deal of power in the state by providing racetrack jobs for distribution as patronage by state legislators.[26] In Utah, where mining is a principal industry and the
Kennecott Copper Corporation is the largest single taxpayer,[27] mining interests rank high among the most powerful lobbies. Oregon's
economy is also dominated by one industry, the lumber industry,
which employs about two thirds of the state's industrial workers
and contributes about two thirds of the state's manufacturing
payroll.[28] It is not surprising, then, that lobbyists in Oregon rank
the lumber industry as a powerful lobby. It is surprising, however,
that *legislators* in Oregon do not include lumber among the ten most
powerful groups. It may be that the economy of the state is so
dependent on the lumber industry—that what is good for the lumber industry is so often good for the state too—that legislators
usually find themselves in agreement with lumber lobbyists apparently of their own accord, without any perceptible exercise of power
on the part of the lobbyist. The same thing might be said in the
cases of the Mormon Church in Utah and the Roman Catholic
Church in Massachusetts.

In our study we also asked legislators to list those groups from
which they received the most pressure. We then ranked these
groups based on the number of times they were mentioned. We now
had three sorts of data: (1) the rankings of groups considered the
most powerful, (2) the rankings of groups considered to apply the
most pressure, and (3) the rankings of groups that are the most
heavily represented. Spearman Rank Order Correlations (r_s) were
performed for each state between the ranking of power and the
other two measures.[29] In every state we found a significant correla-

---

[26] See Lockard, pp. 168–170. Lockard estimates that 85 percent of jobs at
Massachusetts racetracks are distributed by legislators. Requests for these jobs
were running so high that in 1954 the legislature passed a law specifically
''making it a crime for a public official to attempt to use his influence in land-
ing a track job'' (Lockard). This, apparently, neither stopped the legislators
from distributing the jobs nor reduced the power of the racing lobby, which
still ranks among the ten most powerful interest groups in Massachusetts.

[27] Jonas, p. 283.

[28] Swarthout, p. 252.

[29] The Spearman correlation is a statistical measure which enables us to study
the variation in rankings of one set of data with another. If each interest group
ranked in the same order on measures of both power and pressure—that is, if
the most powerful group also applied the most pressure, the second most power-

tion between the power of the group as perceived by the legislators and the number of lobbyists representing the group (Table 2.13). As the number of lobbyists representing the group increased, so did the legislators' perception of the power of the group. This may be an indication that, in the minds of legislators, lobbyists' power and lobbyists' visibility are blurred together. Called upon to name his state's most powerful interest group, a legislator might name the first group that came to mind, and the first group that comes to mind is likely to be one that is heavily represented and thus highly visible.

TABLE 2.13

Spearman Rank Correlations (r_s) between Power
and (1) Application of Pressure, (2) Representation

	APPLICATION OF PRESSURE r_s	*Significance Level*	REPRESENTATION r_s	*Significance Level*
Massachusetts	.11	NS	.43	.01
North Carolina	.11	NS	.38	.02
Oregon	.11	NS	.32	.05
Utah	.15	NS	.25	.08

In none of the states did we find a significant correlation between power and amount of pressure applied. There are, however, in spite of the absence of overall correlations, noticeable correlations in particular cases. For instance, education in Utah and labor generally are usually viewed as simultaneously powerful and pressure oriented. But, in general, the application of "pressure" upon legislators apparently produces no power for an interest group and therefore is an ineffective means of lobbying.

---

ful group also applied the second most pressure, and so on—then we would get a Spearman correlation of 1.0. We would say there was a perfect relationship between pressure and power. However, if the most powerful group was perceived to apply the least pressure and the second most powerful group the next to the least pressure, and so on down the line, we would get a Spearman correlation of −1.0. We would say this was a perfect inverse relationship: as pressure increases, power decreases, and vice versa. If there is no co-variance, if power and pressure are not related, we would expect a correlation of 0.0.

Environment and the Strengths of Groups

On the basis of a variety of questions administered to legislators and lobbyists, we concluded that interest groups have more impact upon the legislative process in Oregon and Utah than they do in Massachusetts and North Carolina.[30] In the light of this conclusion, it appears that environmental factors, though they do have an effect on the strengths of particular interest groups in particular states, have little effect on the strength of interest groups as a whole. In other words, with regard to the strength of interest groups, environmental variables are randomly distributed. The "weak-lobby" states—Massachusetts and North Carolina—have little in common. Massachusetts is urban, heterogeneous, industrialized, and has a relatively wealthy, well-educated population. North Carolina is the reverse. Massachusetts, furthermore, has a competitive political structure; North Carolina does not. Indeed, Massachusetts is more similar in its degree of party competition to the "strong-lobby" states—Utah and Oregon—than it is to North Carolina. Utah and Oregon have more in common than Massachusetts and North Carolina, though on a variety of measures Utah and Oregon are approximations of Massachusetts.

Mobility of population is the only characteristic which varies consistently with interest-group strength. The populations of strong-lobby states display greater mobility than the populations of weak-lobby states. Mobility, however, is in reality an artifact of a more fundamental distinction between weak- and strong-lobby states, a distinction which is more developmental than environmental. To illustrate this point, let us add to our sample temporarily two states examined by Wahlke, Eulau, Buchanan, and Ferguson: California, which is clearly a strong-lobby state, and Tennessee, which is clearly a weak-lobby state.[31] We can now see that there is a basic distinction to be made between newer, late-developing states and older, now-established political systems. By the time interest groups had begun to develop in Massachusetts, Tennessee, and North Carolina, the rules of the game of politics had been established, and, in a sense, the game had been closed to interest groups.

[30] For a discussion in detail of the findings that led to this conclusion, see Chapter 7.

[31] Ohio and New Jersey—also examined by Wahlke and his colleagues—are excluded here because their classification is less certain.

In the southern states, legislators are likely to view all "outsiders" (interest groups, parties, constituents) as having doubtful legitimacy. In Massachusetts, interest groups have a difficult time competing with established parties. Each of these states, in other words, is characterized by an oligarchical type of politics which operates to exclude interest groups.

In the western states, however, political systems and interest groups developed simultaneously. Interest groups did not have to fight existing political institutions; they shared in the development of the political system; lobbyists and politicians "grew up" together. Furthermore, the political traditions of the western states —nonpartisanship, open primaries, a high rate of participation— invite interest groups (along with everybody else) to compete for the stakes of politics.

A further possible explanation for the relative strengths of interest groups is raised by this notion of the stakes of politics. We should consider the obvious possibility that interest groups will be attracted to arenas where important decisions are being made—the arenas where the stakes are the biggest. Do the stakes vary from state to state? Do some states do a "bigger business" than others? If so, how does this relate to patterns of group politics? In order to answer these questions, we compiled Table 2.14, which compares the per-capita revenues and expenditures of the strong- and the weak-lobby states. Clearly, the strong-lobby states have a greater economic output than the weak-lobby states. The research of Dye, Hofferbert, and others mentioned earlier suggests that environment influences output.[32] Here we have found a variation on this suggestion: The magnitude of the output influences the pattern of activity accompanying the output.

TABLE 2.14

Expenditures and Revenues of Strong- and Weak-Lobby States

| | STRONG-LOBBY STATES | | | WEAK-LOBBY STATES | | |
	Oregon	California	Utah	Massa-chusetts	Tennessee	North Carolina
Revenue: per capita	$257	$251	$251	$185	$171	$183
Expenditure: per capita	260	254	255	190	164	171

[32] See Chapter 1, note 13.

3 THE GROUNDWORK FOR INTERACTION

Legislators and lobbyists are, in a restricted sense of the word, members of elite groups. Legislators have been selected from the general population and have been assigned a position of limited authority with institutionalized powers. Lobbyists, although they have not undergone a formal process of popular selection, have been recruited by politically active groups with the expectation (or hope) that they can play some role in the decision-making process. Hence, though they are not representatives of geographical districts, lobbyists sometimes do represent large numbers of people. Legislators attach considerable significance to this representative function of lobbyists; those lobbyists who speak for organizations with large memberships are frequently considered to be very powerful.[1] That both legislators and lobbyists may be thought of as representatives suggests the notion of two consultative elites, each contributing a portion of its resources to the resolution or perpetuation of political conflict.

To characterize legislators and lobbyists as members of elites, however, is to imply no more than that they are both engaging in concentrated political activities. It is therefore feasible to conceptualize the lobbying process in terms of an interaction or exchange between two groups of people highly active in politics. The point of this chapter is to ascertain what characteristics each partner brings into this interaction from his life prior to the beginning of his political activity.

[1] See pp. 194–197.

The Notion of Overlap

Introductory interactions are extremely important in determining the future of relationships.[2] This first interaction between any two partners is tentative and exploratory. Neither partner is sure what to expect of the other and neither has much more than a stereotypic image of the other. Consequently, the background of each partner is likely to be of prime importance until a new frame of reference (such as an institutionalized role) is developed. Having no experiential evidence as to the likely outcome of an initial interaction, both partners will rely upon previous experience to organize their perceptions. It should be kept in mind that the exchange between legislators and lobbyists is not entirely free or equal: The necessity for interaction is greater for lobbyists. Nevertheless, similarity or dissimilarity in background should help us to understand the nature of the legislator-lobbyist exchange, since, as numerous studies have demonstrated, people tend to interact most often and most freely with people similar to themselves.[3]

The initial interaction will be facilitated if legislators and lobbyists begin the exchange with at least a partially correct understanding of what the other "stands for." As an illustration of this point, let us imagine a communication situation involving people with almost completely disparate backgrounds. Campbell and Hepler describe the situation of an aviator forced to parachute from his aircraft over Australia.[4] After descending safely and extricating himself from the parachute, he looks up to see an aborigine threatening him with a spear. In order to save his life, the aviator must communicate with the aborigine and must in turn be able to understand the messages transmitted by the aborigine. Since neither partner knows the language of the other and since both partners are products of quite dissimilar cultures, communication will be extremely difficult. Other than the fact that they are both human beings, they have very little common background upon which to base an interaction. If we think of a pair of partially overlapping

---

[2] Peter M. Blau, *Exchange and Power in Social Life* (New York: John Wiley, 1964), pp. 33–59.

[3] See, for example, John W. Thibaut and Harold H. Kelley, *The Social Psychology of Groups* (New York: John Wiley, 1961), p. 48.

[4] James H. Campbell and Hal W. Hepler, "Persuasion and Interpersonal Relations," in Campbell and Hepler, eds., *Dimensions in Communication* (Belmont, Calif.: Wadsworth Publishing Co., 1965), p. 89.

circles as a model for interaction, each circle representing a man
and the amount of overlap between the circles representing the
knowledge and experience that the two men hold in common, the
aborigine-aviator interaction would present us with two circles with
very little overlap.[5]

Of course, interaction is seldom required of people having so
little in common as an aborigine and an aviator. Most interaction
occurs between partners possessing at least some cultural or personal experience in common. On the other hand, it is impossible to
imagine an interaction in a situation of complete overlap. Such a
situation is most nearly approximated in a case of identical twins
reared in the same environment, but even identical twins are not
similar in every respect. In the everyday world of interactions, the
amount of overlap varies between these two extremes; that is to say,
overlap is never as great as for identical twins nor as incomplete as
for an aviator and an aborigine. Within these parameters, the
greater the degree of overlap, the better the possibility that each
partner can predict the responses of the other. Prediction of the
responses of another is one of the keys to becoming an ''effective
communicator,'' and, since the goal of the lobbyist is to become an
effective communicator, it is relevant to know the degree of overlap
between legislators and lobbyists.

The Socioeconomic Status of Legislators and Lobbyists

Studies of American officeholders have by now dispelled the ''log
cabin'' myth of open political mobility. Although there are many
examples of individuals of low socioeconomic status achieving political office, it is, on the whole, usually the well-educated, middle- or
upper-income, professional person who is elected to office. It is true,
of course, that mere membership in a class does not guarantee that
an individual will automatically reflect the values ascribed to the
class. Other factors, such as institutional office, frequently intervene

---

[5] As in the case of the aviator and the aborigine, the outcome of interaction
may be—quite literally—a matter of life and death. Such extreme outcomes
are certainly not characteristic of legislator-lobbyist interaction, although,
occasionally, group survival is *perceived* to be at stake. Labor lobbyists, for
example, may perceive group survival to be threatened by ''right-to-work''
legislation.

to modify an individual's class-linked attitudes. Nevertheless, people with similar socioeconomic backgrounds should have an easier time interacting than those without such similarities in their backgrounds.

By one criterion, median family income, the backgrounds of legislators and lobbyists are quite similar (see Table 3.1). The difference between the median family incomes of legislators and lobbyists is quite small compared to the difference between the income of either of these two groups and the income of the general

TABLE 3.1

Median Family Incomes of Legislators,
Lobbyists, and General Population

	Legislators	Lobbyists	General Population
Massachusetts	$13,048	$12,420	$6,272
North Carolina	18,545	18,445	3,956
Oregon	13,755	11,772	5,892
Utah	10,214	11,384	5,899

population. In three of the states legislators earn slightly more than lobbyists; in the fourth state, Utah, lobbyists earn just a bit more than legislators. In neither case, however, can it be argued that these minor differences indicate a fundamental difference in style of life.

The educational level of both legislators and lobbyists is also quite high in comparison to the general population (see Tables 3.2 and 3.3). As in the case of income, the difference in educational level between the two elites is quite small in comparison to the gulf between the elites and the general population. Notice, however, that there is a slight tendency for more lobbyists than legislators to have completed college. Thus, lobbyists, though slightly less highly paid, are a somewhat more highly educated group than legislators.

The disparities in both income and educational attainment between the two elite groups and the general population are greatest in North Carolina. While the general population in North Carolina has the lowest median family income and the lowest level of education of any of the four states, the elite population has the highest income and the highest educational level of any of the states. The unusually high level of education and income of legislators and

TABLE 3.2

Education of Legislators and Lobbyists

	Completed High School	Program Beyond High School	Completed College	Graduate or Professional School	(N)
MASSACHUSETTS					
Legislators	98%	70%	56%	35%	(244)
Lobbyists	95	74	62	32	(185)
NORTH CAROLINA					
Legislators	96	87	64	44	(164)
Lobbyists	95	85	73	63	(132)
OREGON					
Legislators	95	77	54	39	(84)
Lobbyists	93	77	59	36	(193)
UTAH					
Legislators	92	78	57	31	(90)
Lobbyists	95	81	62	41	(134)

lobbyists in North Carolina is possibly a function of that state's relatively closed opportunity structure. Schlesinger's ranking of general opportunity levels places North Carolina, along with Massachusetts, considerably below Oregon, which in turn is ranked below Utah.[6] Thus, it apparently takes quite a bit of money and education to get involved in the political process in North Carolina. Interestingly, although Massachusetts has an equally difficult opportunity structure, money and education do not seem to be as crucial to political success there as they are in North Carolina. A possible

TABLE 3.3

Proportion of the Population Completing
High School and College (Persons over 25)

	High School	College
Massachusetts	47%	9%
North Carolina	32	6
Oregon	48	8
Utah	56	10

[6] Joseph Schlesinger, *Ambition and Politics* (Chicago: Rand McNally & Co., 1966), p. 51.

explanation for this is that the strong political parties in Massachusetts serve to constrict the entry of potential activists, just as does
the traditionalist and relatively rigid opportunity structure of
North Carolina.

Current occupation is the third usual component of an estimate
of socioeconomic status. One might think the facts here are obvious
—that the current occupation of the sample is either legislator or
lobbyist—but such is not always the case. Politics at the state level
is considerably more amateurish than national politics. While one
normally thinks of Senator Fulbright and Representative Ford as a
senator and a representative respectively, one hardly considers state
legislators as making a full-time career of their legislative functions. The pay is too low and the amount of time consumed is too
little. Whereas most national politicians realize a substantial portion of their income from their legislative position, few state legislators do so. This is even more true of lobbyists. Since in most cases
the legislative session lasts only a few months (Massachusetts being
the notable exception), lobbyists must have other sources of income.
Some lobbyists, therefore, are association executives who devote a
portion of their time to lobbying; others are public relations con-
sultants who spend the "off-season" handling commercial and political accounts; still others are lawyers on retainer who maintain a
normal practice when the legislature is not in session; and a few,
whose lobbying experience is usually limited to a single session,
have occupations essentially unrelated to their lobbying function.

From what we have learned about the income and educational
characteristics of legislators and lobbyists, we would assume that
their extra-political occupations are of a relatively high status.[7]
Such is, indeed, the case (see Table 3.4). Most legislators and
lobbyists either are lawyers or occupy another professional or managerial position of similar status. There is a slight tendency (most
pronounced in Oregon and Utah) for legislators to come from
professional and managerial ranks in greater proportion than lobbyists. Surprisingly, the proportion of lawyers is in some cases not
as great as the proportion of professional and managerial personnel
without legal training. The pattern is not clear for lobbyists, but,
among legislators, professional and managerial personnel without
legal training far outnumber lawyers in Oregon and Utah. In

[7] See Ronald D. Hedlund and Samuel C. Patterson, "Personal Attributes,
Political Orientations, and Occupational Perspectives of Lobbyists: The Case
of Illinois," *Iowa Business Digest*, 37 (November 1966), 3–11.

Massachusetts and North Carolina the proportions are roughly the same. Utah is unusually low in the proportion of both legislators and lobbyists who are lawyers. Utah is low not only in comparison with the states in this sample, but also in comparison with other

TABLE 3.4

Current Occupations of Legislators and Lobbyists

	Legislators	Lobbyists
PROFESSIONALS AND MANAGERS, OTHER THAN LAWYERS		
Massachusetts	27%	27%
North Carolina	31	26
Oregon	38	23
Utah	45	38
LAWYERS		
Massachusetts	26	21
North Carolina	37	42
Oregon	24	19
Utah	9	10
LABOR		
Massachusetts	3	9
North Carolina	1	5
Oregon	5	16
Utah	7	15
FARMERS		
Massachusetts	0	1
North Carolina	13	2
Oregon	11	3
Utah	14	6
CLERKS AND SALESMEN		
Massachusetts	17	6
North Carolina	4	6
Oregon	11	9
Utah	10	9

states examined in previous studies, which suggest that, nationally, at least one fourth of all legislators are lawyers.[8] Much has been written about the natural affinity of the legal profession and political life. This is the case not only because lawyers have more time and more flexible schedules than do many other professionals and because lawyers better understand the legal terminology in which

[8] Heinz Eulau and John D. Sprague, *Lawyers in Politics* (Indianapolis: Bobbs-Merrill Co., 1964), p. 12.

legislation is couched, but also because lawyers are quickly socialized into the political process due to the combative and yet conciliatory nature of their profession.[9]

The surprising aspect of these data is not the dominance of lawyers but the fact that in some states legal training is apparently not as important as one would expect. Contrast, for example, Utah and North Carolina. Here again, one is tempted to draw upon the Schlesinger analysis of low- and high-opportunity states. By this analysis, Utah appears to be a much less traditionalist state with less restricted access to political office than is the case in North Carolina. Thus, legal skills are not as great a resource in Utah and there are fewer lawyers in the legislature of that state. There is the further possibility that institutional forces other than the legal profession dominate the Utah political process. The one force that comes most readily to mind, of course, is the Mormon Church. A vast majority of Utah legislators are, in fact, Mormon bishops and have spent a portion of their time as missionaries. The "normal" method of entry into Utah politics appears to be through the institutional structure of the church rather than through the legal profession.

The substantial state-by-state variations in the occupational backgrounds of legislators and lobbyists should not obscure the fact that variations in one group are accompanied by variations in the other. Thus, North Carolina has the highest proportion of lawyers among both legislators and lobbyists, while Utah has the lowest proportion among both groups. Therefore, legislators and lobbyists are, within the specific environment in which they function, quite similar in occupational background.

Career Mobility

There is one characteristic of the occupational backgrounds of legislators and lobbyists, however, which is quite dissimilar: career mobility. It has frequently been argued that legislators are upwardly mobile in their career aspirations.[10] Our data are unable to comment upon vertical mobility, but we can speculate that it is

---

[9] Eulau and Sprague, pp. 87–88.

[10] See, for instance, Thomas R. Dye, "State Legislative Politics," in Herbert Jacob and Kenneth N. Vines, eds., *Politics in the American States* (Boston: Little, Brown and Co., 1965), p. 167.

much more likely that legislators would use their positions for
further political (or perhaps professional or business) advancement
than lobbyists would. Though the legislator may think of his job as
the beginning or middle point of a career pattern, there is virtually
no evidence to suggest that lobbyists begin their careers with expectations of advancing beyond lobbying to a political office or to a
more lucrative nonpolitical occupation. On the other hand, the
career of the lobbyist is characterized by substantial horizontal
mobility. While about one third of the legislators of our sample had
nonpolitical occupations prior to their election to the legislature,
fully 85 percent of the lobbyists had nonpolitical occupations before
being hired to lobby. Lobbyists appear to be able to move easily
from job to job, not necessarily in a drifting fashion, but certainly
with considerably less commitment to a given occupation than is
characteristic of legislators. Their occupational pattern suggests
more flexibility, perhaps more risk-taking, than does the pattern for
legislators. Occupationally speaking, lobbyists have "been around"
quite a bit more than legislators.

Career Motivations

Given the differences in the mobility patterns of the careers of
lobbyists and legislators, we might expect to find corresponding
differences in their motivations for beginning their careers. Indeed,
there is good reason to suspect *a priori* that the decision on the part
of an individual to become a legislator is not at all similar to a
decision to become a lobbyist. To begin with, the career of a legislator is a more visible, socially acceptable way of playing the game of
politics. Though state legislators are not exceptionally high on any
measure of social status, they are probably higher than lobbyists.
The average person seeking a career in politics would probably
think of becoming a legislator rather than a lobbyist. The occupation of the lobbyist, furthermore, has many of the characteristics of
marginality.[11] A marginal occupation is an imperfectly institutionalized one; there is some ambiguity in the pattern of behavior
expected of a person filling the occupational role. Marginal occupational roles, such as those of the chiropractor, the professional

---

[11] For a discussion of marginality, see Walter I. Wardwell, "The Reduction
of Strain on a Marginal Social Role," *American Journal of Sociology*, 61 (July
1955), 16–25.

gambler, and (prior to the 1930s) the labor organizer are not likely to attract persons with a clear image of the expectations attached to the role. Persons entering the occupation, therefore, are less likely to be doing so out of predetermined choice. For example, there is evidence that there is less of a conscious choice in becoming a chiropractor than in becoming a medical doctor. Many chiropractors originally intended to be medical doctors.

We would expect, then, less of a tendency for lobbyists than for legislators to plan their careers. Studies of legislators have produced some useful categories for analysis of the motivations for beginning a legislative career. For purposes of comparison with lobbyists, a particularly useful distinction is whether the legislator is a "self-starter" or was encouraged to run either by friends, interest groups, or party organizations.[12] Self-starters generally enter politics for "moral" reasons—for instance, to improve the community or to advance the cause of a specific endeavor, such as education or mental health. Legislators who are persuaded to run by other factors, while they can hardly be described as without conviction, seem to be less ideologically committed than self-starters. Given the difference in the nature of legislating and lobbying and the difference in the mobility patterns of the careers of legislators and lobbyists, it is quite likely that relatively few lobbyists are "self-starters." That is to say, few lobbyists actually made a decision to become lobbyists in the same way one decides to become a doctor, lawyer, or teacher. It is true that, retrospectively, some lobbyists claim to have made such a decision, but these are relatively very few.

In Table 3.5 we have tabulated the responses of legislators and lobbyists when asked whether they were self-recruited, persuaded to enter the occupation by others (co-opted), or simply drifted into the occupation. In every state, legislators tend to be self-starters and lobbyists tend to be drifters. Quite similar to the "drift" response is the response of lobbyists that they were prevailed upon by friends and associates to assume the role of lobbyist. While not as indeterminate as those in the "drift" category, lobbyists who give this response are also indicating a lack of clear intention.

In sum, the planned-on, ideologically inspired character of the legislator's career pattern stands in clear contrast to the indetermi-

---

[12] See Lester G. Seligman, "Recruitment in Politics," *PROD*, 1 (1958), 14–17.

TABLE 3.5

Entry Mechanisms of Legislators and Lobbyists*

	Self-Recruited	Co-opted	Drifted	(N)
MASSACHUSETTS				
Legislators	70%	17	17	(244)
Lobbyists	38%	30	86	(185)
NORTH CAROLINA				
Legislators	61%	23	22	(164)
Lobbyists	19%	44	91	(132)
OREGON				
Legislators	62%	35	20	(84)
Lobbyists	20%	46	79	(193)
UTAH				
Legislators	60%	42	18	(90)
Lobbyists	33%	50	85	(134)

* Total percentages exceed 100 because of multiple responses.

nate character of the lobbyist's pattern. The following are typical responses to an inquiry about how one becomes a lobbyist.

> I don't know. My training was in news work. I don't know how I got into lobbying and I don't know how I got into trade association work. If I look back and wonder how in hell I got here, it's a mystery to me.

> I was running the public relations arm of some insurance company, and as a result of this I was hired as an assistant executive secretary of the insurance association. Part of the job was, I subsequently learned, saving them from spending twenty-five hundred bucks for the lawyer they had on retainer. Prior to this I had done some one-shot work in another state. If somebody had offered me a job as a lobbyist, I would have told them they were out of their skull. I just kind of fell into it.

Although they are by far in the minority, some lobbyists are self-starters. Though seldom general ideologues, self-starting lobbyists are likely to have sought their position primarily to help a single cause. They are likely to be more committed to that cause than to the occupation of lobbyist. Furthermore, their relations with their colleagues are less "professional" and more competitive than are those of lobbyists who were persuaded to become lobbyists by others or who drifted into the occupation.

Age of Politicization

Given the clearer career commitment of legislators, we would expect them to remember an earlier interest than lobbyists in entering their occupation. If a person is self-recruited, as most legislators are, it is likely that he began to give his career consideration relatively early in life. If, on the other hand, a person is fulfilling an occupational role because of reasons that are unclear even to himself, it is likely that he did not give serious thought to the job until just before he accepted it. The data confirm these expectations. In every state a majority of legislators, in contrast to a tiny fraction of lobbyists, recall being interested in a political career prior to the age of twenty (Table 3.6). Notice, however, that Massa-

TABLE 3.6

Percentage of Legislators and Lobbyists Whose Earliest
Recollection of Interest in Politics Is before Age 20

	Massa-chusetts % (N)	North Carolina % (N)	Oregon % (N)	Utah % (N)	Total % (N)
Legislators	54.1 (244)	70.1 (164)	57.1 (84)	74.5 (90)	52.2 (582)
Lobbyists	15.6 (185)	10.6 (132)	10.3 (193)	7.7 (134)	10.3 (644)

chusetts lobbyists, just as they are more likely to be self-starters than lobbyists in other states, are also more likely to display an earlier interest in lobbying.

The relationship between motivations for entry and recollections of first interest provides a final way of contrasting the career patterns of legislators and lobbyists. Self-entry should be related to early recollections of interest among both legislators and lobbyists. Even though there are few self-starters among lobbyists, those that are self-starters should be substantially more likely to indicate an earlier interest in lobbying. The data in Table 3.7 indicate this is generally the case, especially (once again) in Massachusetts. Here, 80 percent of the lobbyists who are self-starters were interested in lobbying before the age of twenty, as compared to less than 40 percent in the other states. Among legislators, the percentages are also proportionately higher in Massachusetts than in other states.

although the differences are not as great. The data suggest that there is an ideological component to Massachusetts lobbying which is absent in other states—a suggestion which can be made more explicit as we examine patterns of interaction in future chapters.

TABLE 3.7

Relationship between Age of First
Interest in Politics and Entry Mechanism

	Percent Self-Starting			
	Legislators		Lobbyists	
Age of Interest	(N)		(N)	
MASSACHUSETTS				
Under 20	83	(132)	80	(26)
20–24	66	(60)	39	(31)
Over 24	55	(47)	29	(104)
NORTH CAROLINA				
Under 20	78	(81)	31	(13)
20–24	71	(84)	17	(12)
Over 24	35	(48)	13	(98)
OREGON				
Under 20	60	(48)	30	(17)
20–24	38	(13)	42	(17)
Over 24	51	(23)	17	(140)
UTAH				
Under 20	58	(43)	40	(10)
20–24	75	(24)	57	(16)
Over 24	50	(22)	31	(104)

Governmental Occupations as Channels of Recruitment

Another dimension of the differences between the careers of legislators and lobbyists is found in the proportion of members of each group who have held governmental positions prior to becoming legislators or lobbyists (see Table 3.8). Looking first at legislators, we note that the proportion of legislators who have had prior governmental experience is substantially smaller in Oregon and Utah than in Massachusetts and North Carolina. This finding is in general support of Schlesinger's suggestion that the opportunity structures of Oregon and Utah are less rigid than those of Massachusetts and North Carolina. Within a more open opportunity structure, we would expect more political amateurism; that is, we would expect less political experience on the parts of individuals occupying political offices in Oregon and Utah. The relationship between amateurism and the behavior of interest groups will be

TABLE 3.8

Percentage of Legislators and Lobbyists Who
Have Held a Previous Governmental Position

	Legislators	(N)	Lobbyists	(N)
Massachusetts	54%	(244)	32%	(185)
North Carolina	58	(164)	61	(132)
Oregon	43	(84)	39	(193)
Utah	37	(90)	51	(134)

explored in a future chapter. At this point it is sufficient to observe that the amateurism of legislators in Oregon and Utah is matched by the relatively strong positions of interest groups in these two states.

We found no clear relationship, however, between the previous governmental experience of lobbyists and the strength of interest groups. The state with the highest percentage of lobbyists with previous governmental experience is North Carolina, a weak-lobby state. The state with the second highest percentage is Utah, a strong-lobby state. We also found no relationship between the percentage of lobbyists with previous governmental experience and the percentage of legislators with previous experience. In Massachusetts very few lobbyists have held governmental positions in comparison to legislators; in North Carolina and Oregon the proportions are roughly comparable; in Utah the proportion is heavily in favor of the lobbyists. The relatively high experience of Utah lobbyists can be linked to the relative inexperience of Utah legislators.[13] This disparity between the resources of legislators and lobbyists in Utah will help us to understand some of the curiosities in the behavior of the Utah respondents. We note elsewhere that although Utah legislators seem to have a rather high distrust of lobbyists, they depend on them rather heavily for information.[14]

[13] See pp. 60–61.
[14] See pp. 106–109.

Perhaps one explanation for this discrepancy between attitudes and behavior is the proportionately greater governmental experience of the Utah lobbyists, as compared to the relative amateurism of the Utah legislators.

In spite of these interstate variations in the number of legislators and lobbyists with previous governmental experience, there is a consistent pattern in the kinds of positions previously held by those who do have experience. Most legislators who have held previous governmental positions have held them at the local level. Most lobbyists who have held previous positions, on the other hand, have held them at the state level or even the national level[15] (see Table 3.9). This pattern suggests a difference for legislators and lobbyists

TABLE 3.9

Types of Governmental Positions
Held by Legislators and Lobbyists

	Local	State	National	(N)*
MASSACHUSETTS				
Legislators	80%	15	4	(184)
Lobbyists	45%	40	14	(77)
NORTH CAROLINA				
Legislators	70%	20	10	(158)
Lobbyists	21%	58	21	(120)
OREGON				
Legislators	57%	31	12	(51)
Lobbyists	20%	57	23	(101)
UTAH				
Legislators	54%	29	17	(48)
Lobbyists	27%	40	33	(82)

* Total number of positions held. This N may exceed the number of respondents holding a governmental position because more than one position may have been held by a respondent.

in the nature of the experience provided by the holding of a previous governmental position. For the legislator, a prior position is likely to have served as a training experience; it is likely to have provided him with a period of political apprenticeship. For the lobbyist, a previous position is likely to have served as a socialization experience, a period during which he became acquainted with

[15] See Hedlund and Patterson, p. 7, for comparable findings.

the machinations of interest groups or became aware of their existence for the first time. Futhermore, most legislators who have held previous governmental positions are likely to have held elective positions, while most lobbyists with previous governmental experience are likely to have held appointive positions. Presumably, the skills demanded of local elected officials are substantially different from those demanded of state or national appointed officials.

In sum, then, the occupational backgrounds of legislators and lobbyists can be considered quite dissimilar. Perhaps this disparity explains the fact that, contrary to myth, there is relatively little interchange between the positions of legislator and lobbyist. Only a small proportion of lobbyists have ever been legislators and only an even smaller proportion of legislators have ever been lobbyists.[16] At any rate, in the light of the more subtle dissimilarity in their occupational backgrounds, the similarity in the socioeconomic backgrounds of legislators and lobbyists is devalued in importance. An understanding of the fundamentally different paths of entry into their respective occupations now becomes essential in understanding the resources and images that each partner brings into interaction.

Backgrounds of Business and Labor Lobbyists

We would be in error if we continued to examine lobbyists as though they were a homogeneous collection of individuals. Because they are selected explicitly to represent potentially conflicting interests, we would expect to find more divergence in the backgrounds of individual lobbyists than in those of individual legislators. We have noted the predominance of business lobbyists in the interest-group systems of all the states.[17] We have also noted the predominance of both legislators and lobbyists with business or professional backgrounds. From these facts, some obvious inferences about the bias of a pressure system can be made. In a business-oriented environment, those groups which are not part of the business main-

16 About 5 percent of lobbyists have been state legislators. The highest percentage (11) occurs in North Carolina.

17 See also Harmon Zeigler, ''Interest Groups in the States,'' in Herbert Jacob and Kenneth N. Vines, eds., *Politics in the American States* (Boston: Little, Brown and Co., 1965), p. 112.

stream are at a disadvantage. The most clearly established competi-
tor to business hegemony is organized labor. Ideologically speaking,
organized labor is certainly waging an uphill battle. The ideological
stance of labor and the class-oriented structure of the movement
make it extremely probable that labor lobbyists will have less in
common with legislators than will business lobbyists. Business lobbyists have the advantage in other ways as well. Consider, for
example, the median family incomes of business and labor lobbyists
(Table 3.10). In every case, labor lobbyists make substantially less

TABLE 3.10

Median Family Incomes of Business and Labor Lobbyists

	Business (N)		Labor (N)	
Massachusetts	$18,909	(50)	$12,231	(13)
Oregon	16,793	(98)	10,152	(33)
Utah	15,931	(54)	8,179	(14)
North Carolina	(Excluded because of lack of labor lobbyists.)			

than business lobbyists. Furthermore, while the overwhelming majority of business lobbyists have completed college, only a minority
of labor lobbyists in the states under consideration have achieved
this educational level (see Table 3.11). Thus, not only are business
lobbyists more similar to legislators in terms of occupation, they
also bear a clearer resemblance to legislators in terms of education.
Only in terms of income are labor lobbyists reasonably similar to
legislators. In short, except in the case of income, overlap is sub-

TABLE 3.11

Percentage of Business and Labor
Lobbyists Who Have Completed College

	Business (N)		Labor (N)	
Massachusetts	82%	(50)	39%	(13)
Oregon	71	(98)	21	(33)
Utah	57	(54)	14	(14)
North Carolina	(Excluded because of lack of labor lobbyists.)			

stantially less for labor lobbyists and legislators than for business lobbyists and legislators, making the task of interaction more difficult for labor lobbyists.

Business lobbyists are also more likely to have held a previous governmental position than are labor lobbyists (see Table 3.12). This tendency is probably a result of American society's overall recruitment pattern, which draws disproportionately from business classes for governmental positions. However, this societal bias in favor of recruitment from the business community is apparently

TABLE 3.12

Percentage of Business and Labor Lobbyists
Who Have Held Previous Governmental Positions

	Business (N)		Labor (N)	
Massachusetts	40%	(50)	15%	(13)
Oregon	45	(98)	27	(33)
Utah	44	(54)	29	(14)
North Carolina	(Excluded because of lack of labor lobbyists.)			

greater at the state and local levels than at the national level. We know that the tendency is for lobbyists in general to have had more governmental experience at the state level than legislators have had. However, there is a substantial difference in the kind of governmental experience of business and labor lobbyists. For example, substantially more business lobbyists have held local or state offices. The governmental experience of labor lobbyists is more likely to have been at the federal level (see Table 3.13). Further, in no state has a labor lobbyist ever held an elective position, whereas the percentage of business lobbyists who have done so ranges from 8 percent in Oregon to 24 percent in Massachusetts. Thus, not only have more business than labor lobbyists held public office, but more of them held offices similar to the offices held by legislators.

Because of their greater federal experience, labor lobbyists are somewhat more "cosmopolitan" than business lobbyists. Furthermore, more labor lobbyists than business lobbyists have had experience in other state legislatures. Thus, because of the nature of the labor movement, more state labor lobbyists than state business lobbyists are likely to have continued contact and interaction with

lobbyists in other states and lobbyists at the federal level. Nevertheless, the deviant position of labor in the American society makes the
job of the state labor lobbyist especially tedious. Indeed, the job
requires a rather high level of commitment. We have noted that
lobbyists tend to drift into their jobs without much previous consideration of the career. This is less true of labor lobbyists than of
business lobbyists. When asked why they became lobbyists, the
majority of labor lobbyists relate their decision to a desire to

TABLE 3.13

Types of Governmental Positions Held
by Business and Labor Lobbyists

	Local	State	National	(N)
MASSACHUSETTS				
Business	12%	22%	10%	(52)
Labor	0	0	15	(13)
OREGON				
Business	6	38	10	(98)
Labor	6	9	18	(33)
UTAH				
Business	13	19	19	(54)
Labor	0	7	21	(14)
NORTH CAROLINA				
		(Excluded because of lack of		
		labor lobbyists.)		

achieve an ideological goal—the goal of helping organized labor—
whereas the majority of business lobbyists speak more in terms of
career opportunities with little mention of ideology. Whereas the
specific events surrounding an individual's decision to become a
labor lobbyist are frequently as ambiguous as the events surrounding the decision of the business lobbyist, it is clear that the entry of
the labor lobbyist into the occupation was preceded by a strong
commitment to the goals of his organization. These differences in
motivation are, at least partially, a consequence of the tendency of
adherents of deviant ideologies to be activists. Deviant ideologies
require a higher, more active level of advocacy.

Ironically, labor lobbyists and legislators are similar in their
ideological orientations. However, given the relative lack of compat-
ibility between labor ideology and legislator ideology, it would
probably be preferable for labor lobbyists to exhibit less commitment to their cause and more flexibility in their positions. A busi-

ness lobbyist's commitment to a business ideology is less visible, because the assumptions of that ideology are generally supported by the members of the decision-making body and, indeed, by the entire political community.

Socialization and Behavior

This examination of the backgrounds of legislators and lobbyists has been undertaken on the assumption (derived from interaction theory) that the extent of overlap in the backgrounds of the participants is helpful in understanding the flow of an interaction. In future chapters, we will relate the concept of interaction to behavioral patterns which, in turn, can be linked to the background variables discussed in this chapter. Beyond the broad assumption that background affects interaction, it is difficult to relate political socialization (the process by which one becomes aware of politics) to current perceptual orientation. Logically speaking, political socialization should be a good predictor of the way a person looks at the world, but, empirically, this is not always the case. For example, Prewitt, Eulau, and Zisk found very little relationship between role orientations and patterns of socialization for legislators and city councilmen.[18] However, they believe that socialization *should* affect the behavior of adults, especially in the area of personal contacts.

Since the major emphasis of this book is on interaction, it was deemed desirable to determine if there are any variations in interaction which can be related to the nature of the political socialization which the legislator or lobbyist undergoes. One of the major variables dealt with by Prewitt, Eulau, and Zisk (and also by us) is the point in the life cycle at which a political career became attractive. Assuming that those whose interest in politics began at an early age are more acculturated toward the give-and-take of day-to-day politics, we might hypothesize that those legislators and lobbyists who were politicized in their youth are more likely than those who were politicized later in life to have high interaction rates with their opposite numbers. This hypothesis could be extended to include interaction with any other possible partner, such as colleagues or constituents. The point is simply that earlier politicization should induce an individual toward higher rates of interaction. For legisla-

[18] Kenneth E. Prewitt, Heinz Eulau, and Betty H. Zisk, ''Political Socialization and Political Roles,'' *Public Opinion Quarterly*, 30 (Winter 1966), 569–581.

tors, this hypothesis works reasonably well. Those legislators who were interested in politics in pre-adult years are more likely than those whose interest began in adulthood to interact with lobbyists. The differences are not great, but the direction is consistent.[19] For lobbyists, however, there is no relationship between age of politicization and interaction with legislators. This absence of relationship among lobbyists can be explained by two facts. First, very few lobbyists had a pre-adult interest in their occupation. Secondly, the occupation of lobbyist is so keyed to interaction with legislators that any personal inclinations based upon pre-adult socialization patterns are muted. As noted earlier, the decision to interact is much freer for legislators than for lobbyists.

We also wished to investigate the possibility of a relationship between legislators' motivations for entry into politics and level of interaction with lobbyists. We noted that most legislators are self-starters and most lobbyists are not. However, among self-starting legislators, we can make a distinction between those whose interest in politics is diffuse and those whose interest in politics is specific. Some self-starting legislators indicate that their interest in a political career is simply to improve the community or to provide general service to the state. Other self-starters, however, indicate they were interested in a more specific aspect of public policy. These legislators actually bear substantial resemblance to lobbyists who have a specific commitment to an organization goal. Legislators whose motivation for a political career is dominated by a generalized desire to improve might be expected to be more hostile to those lobbyists whose commitment to a "general public interest" is not as great as that of the legislator. Our research did find a relationship between a legislator's *motivation* for entry and his attitude toward lobbyists. Those with a diffuse political interest are more hostile than those with a specific interest. Further, we observed a behavioral consequence linked to motivation for entry. Not only do legislators with a specific political interest have a more favorable attitude toward lobbyists, they are also likely to interact with them to a greater degree and are especially more likely to initiate communication with them (see Table 3.14).

---

[19] The differences are substantially greater in Oregon and Utah; in these states about 58 percent of the legislators politicized prior to age 20 are "high interactors," compared to 43 percent of the legislators politicized after age 20. In Massachusetts and North Carolina, the percentages are 41 and 36, respectively.

TABLE 3.14

Legislators' Reason for Entry into the Occupation
and Frequency of Communications (Per
Session) Initiated by Legislators with Lobbyists

Reason for Entry	0–5	6–10	11+	(N)
MASSACHUSETTS				
To serve community	48%	22	30	(60)
Specific interest	23%	23	55	(22)
NORTH CAROLINA				
To serve community	67%	23	13	(39)
Specific interest	61%	17	22	(23)
OREGON				
To serve community	5%	10	85	(20)
Specific interest	6%	19	75	(16)
UTAH				
To serve community	33%	44	23	(18)
Specific interest	17%	50	33	(12)

In future chapters, it will be shown that there is a strong relationship between the extent to which a legislator initiates communication with lobbyists and the extent to which he is influenced by
that communication. Thus, since we can relate willingness to initiate communication with motivations for entry into politics, we can
offer some explanation as to possible background factors which
produce a strong interest-group system. However, factors related to
the arena of decision making itself are more likely to be crucial for
interaction than factors linked to the personal background of the
decision makers. Whereas political socialization apparently influences the extent of interaction between legislators and lobbyists,
this interaction is still further influenced by components of the
general situational context. Granted that the socialization of an
adult affects that adult's view of self and others (especially to the
extent that socialization events predispose a person toward positive
or negative stereotypes of an interaction partner), it is nevertheless
probable that the course of the interaction is not predictable solely
from events which occurred prior to the interaction. Thus, current
self-images can be considered an important aspect of the interaction
process. In this chapter, we have concentrated upon the extent of
the overlap which precedes the interaction. We now turn our attention to images which are more immediate to the interaction and
which control its outcome to a greater extent.

4 THE JOB OF LOBBYING

The character of an interaction is determined initially by
the perceptions that each partner carries with him. An
initial contact is made without any clear understanding
of the characteristics of the other as an individual, and,
hence, stereotypes dominate. However, the interaction is
begun with a fairly clear self-perception. Each person has
an image of himself, an image which may or may not be
congruent with the image of him held by another person.
In this chapter, we will concentrate upon the lobbyist's
self-perception, his view of his job, his view of his responsibilities to his organization and to his fellow lobbyists, his
perception and acceptance of the rules by which the game
of lobbying is played, and his description of the nature of
his daily routine.

Stability in the Occupation

The United States Department of Labor publishes a book,
entitled *Occupational Outlook Handbook,* which "offers a
broadly ranging consideration of almost all the principal
occupational categories in the American economy."[1] The
occupations listed include everything from geophysicist to
waitress, from public relations worker to bus driver. Con-
spicuously absent, however, is any information on the
occupation of lobbyist. Even if we look under some of the

[1] United States Department of Labor, *Occupational Outlook Handbook,* Bulletin No. 1450 (1966–1967), p. iii.

60

numerous euphemisms for lobbyist, such as legislative advocate or legal consultant, there is no occupation listed which bears any resemblance to the job of the lobbyist. The omission of lobbying from the list of occupational choices is not an oversight on the part of the Department of Labor; the Department simply does not consider lobbying part of the "normal" labor market. One can hardly imagine a recruiter for the National Association of Manufacturers appearing on college campuses to compete with representatives of corporations seeking to employ college graduates. Yet, in spite of its role ambiguities, the staying power of the occupation of lobbyist is quite high. Lobbyists tend to remain in the occupation for fairly long periods of time, especially when compared to state legislators (see Table 4.1). In all

TABLE 4.1

Mean Years Experience of Legislators and Lobbyists

	Massachusetts (N)		North Carolina (N)		Oregon (N)		Utah (N)	
Legislators	6.6	(244)	6.2	(164)	6.9	(84)	4.5	(90)
Lobbyists	8.8	(185)	12.3	(132)	8.0	(193)	11.8	(134)

four of the states of this study the mean experience of lobbyists exceeds by far that of legislators. Further, except in Oregon, there are more "freshmen" among legislators than lobbyists and more lobbyists than legislators who have been around for 25 years or more. About 1 percent of the legislators have amassed this much experience, compared to percentages among lobbyists ranging from 4 to 13. Data from other states indicates that there are impressive interstate variations. For example, Patterson found that about 47 percent of Oklahoma lobbyists were registered for the first time at the time of the interview, but that only 11 percent of Illinois lobbyists had served less than two years.[2] It does appear, since the pattern of our four states is consistent, that the lobbyists in our sample are more experienced than the legislators.

The greater experience of lobbyists can be considered a resource which helps to equalize the exchange with legislators. As we shall

[2] Samuel C. Patterson, "The Role of the Lobbyist: The Case of Oklahoma," *Journal of Politics*, 25 (1963), 79. The Illinois data were provided by Professor Patterson.

see, when legislators seek out lobbyists for information, they frequently want, in addition to technical information, estimates of the
probable success of a particular piece of legislation—a "head
count." This is a chore which experienced lobbyists are believed to
be capable of performing. Hence, experienced lobbyists are sought
out by legislators more frequently than "freshmen."

Lobbying: Occupation or Profession?

The greater occupational longevity cannot, however, be taken as
prima facie evidence of greater commitment to the occupation. It
may be that lobbyists continue in this job longer than legislators not
because they desire to, but simply because the restricted mobility
structure of lobbying affords lobbyists fewer opportunities to move
on to a higher position. Furthermore, the longer one remains in a
job the less likely he is to leave it, even if he is not entirely
comfortable in it. These intervening variables make it necessary to
explore the attitudes of lobbyists toward their jobs in greater detail.
The basic dimension of exploration is the concept of a *profession*.
To what extent does the job of lobbyist exhibit characteristics which
are usually attributed to professions?

Sociologists make a distinction between occupations and professions. All occupations strive for professional status. Lobbyists, like
everybody else, like to think of themselves as members of a profession, but this self-image does not take into account the attributes of
professionalism. In reality, all jobs have a place on a continuum
between an ideal occupation and an ideal profession. Greenwood has
extracted from the literature of the sociology of occupations those
attributes which are essential to an ideal profession. Professions are
distinguished by their possession of (1) a systematic theory of the
execution of the duties of the job; (2) authority to perform the job,
authority recognized by the clientele of the profession; (3) community recognition and approval of this authority; (4) a code of ethics
regulating relations with clients and colleagues; and (5) a professional culture sustained by formal organization.[3]

Some of these attributes are obviously lacking in the job of
lobbying. For example, there are no schools where one can study the
theoretical basis of lobbying, nor have there been studies that dis-

---

[3] Ernest Greenwood, "Attributes of a Profession," *Social Work*, 2 (1957),
44–55.

covered any systematic body of knowledge on the part of the lobbyist about the responsibilities of his job. Further, there is little evidence that the community understands, much less approves of, the responsibilities of lobbyists. However, in some degree, portions of the other attributes of a profession are to be found among lobbyists, in some states to a greater degree than in others. To an extent, for example, the lobbyist's clientele does recognize his possession of a certain authority. Informally, the clientele of the lobbyist is both the organization he represents and the legislators with whom he interacts. However, in terms of formal responsibility, only the organization is the clientele of the lobbyist. Lobbyists are not always given authority to participate in organizational policy making, but they are generally allowed to approach the legislature in the way they deem most suitable. The client of the lobbyist usually recognizes that he has hired a person presumed to be capable of making the proper decisions in his dealings with legislators. When this recognition is made, a professional relationship develops, a relationship not unlike that between a lawyer and his client. The client generally establishes a goal and leaves the job of achieving the goal to the lawyer or the lobbyist.

On the other hand, many lobbyists are involved in the decision-making machinery of their organization, especially if they hold an office in the organization but sometimes even if they do not. Lobbyists with long experience and a good reputation are sometimes considered by the organization to be good judges of what is best even with regard to substantive policy. The following comment by a lobbyist, asked what he would do if a bill he was supporting was unfavorably acted upon by a committee, indicates something of the extent of his freedom of action:

> I would wait until the bill came out of committee and then I would talk to the president of the association; that's my boss. But, in effect, he would be likely to do what I suggested.

Such confidence is not, of course, universal. Lobbyists occasionally encounter hostility from their organizations when they are required by the realities of the legislative situation to modify goals without consulting the organization. One lobbyist, who was relatively new at his job and who did not hold an office in the association that employed him, was viewed primarily as an executor of association decisions. Jealous of its authority, but aware of the necessity for flexibility, the association had produced a set of "approved guidelines" for its lobbyists, allowing them to use their own judgment if the occasion required it. Nevertheless, a situation arose in which this lobbyist was not secure in using his judgment. He, as an education lobbyist, was supporting the passage of an educational and professional standards bill to increase the voice of teachers in teacher certification. The bill would have established a certification board consisting entirely of educators. A basic legislative goal of the educational association was that lay members should not be represented on the board. However, within the legislature there was considerable interest in creating a position on the board for a representative of the "public." It became apparent to the lobbyist that the bill would be defeated unless a concession was made and such a position created. Further, the vote was to be taken in committee at such a time as to make it impossible for the lobbyist to consult with the directors of the association. The lobbyist recalls:

> I had to make decisions right on my feet—out of my vest pocket, so to speak. I had to make a decision which was directly opposed to the position taken by the association, and this modification of the association's position caused real concern on the part of one group within the organization. Our membership was very hostile toward me because I had modified a principle that the association had said they would never compromise. I was called before the association and asked why I had sold them down the river. I felt like a Christian standing before the lions. The only thing that I could do was to explain the situation as best I could. However, they were still upset about it.

The lobbyist-client relationship is fundamentally different when the lobbyist is also an officer in the client organization. More than half of the lobbyists we interviewed hold an office in the association they represent (see Table 4.2). Although most lobbyists ultimately

TABLE 4.2

Proportion of Lobbyists Holding Office
in the Organizations They Represent

		(N)
Massachusetts	59%	(185)
North Carolina	62	(132)
Oregon	57	(193)
Utah	78	(134)

do become personally involved in the success or failure of their organization, those who hold an office in the organization are much more likely to feel a personal identification with organizational goals (see Table 4.3). Officeholders are, of course, more likely to be involved in the making of a given decision; hence they would not be as likely to view the implementation of that decision with the detachment of a lawyer. Officeholders, furthermore, unlike other

TABLE 4.3

Percentages of Officeholders and Non-Officeholders Who
Feel a Personal Interest in Goals of the Organization

	Officeholders (N)		Non-Officeholders (N)	
Massachusetts	63%	(109)	61%	(71)
North Carolina	62	(82)	42	(50)
Oregon	65	(110)	52	(82)
Utah	82	(104)	57	(28)

lobbyists, naturally represent only one organization, thus reinforcing their commitment to its goals. In Utah, 78 percent of the lobbyists are association officers, compared to about 59 percent of the lobbyists in other states. As we noted, there is a clear relationship between taking a personal interest in the affairs of the organization and holding an office in that organization. Thus, Utah lobbyists are unusually committed to their organizations.

The commitment of a lobbyist to an organization on a fairly permanent basis can (but need not) inhibit the development of a professional relationship with his colleagues. Lawyers, for example, are anxious to display good feelings toward their courtroom opponents as soon as litigation is over. Lobbyists who are permanently committed to an organization might have more difficulty in the development of such collegial relationships. However, for several reasons, the commitment of the lobbyist to an organization is not incompatible with his commitment to the profession. One basic reason is that having an organizational base tends to produce longevity in lobbying. Association officers tend to remain lobbyists longer than those whose relationship with associations is temporary. Longevity in the occupation, of course, produces greater collegial relations, since interaction between lobbyists increases with lobbying experience. Furthermore, in many cases, the lobbyist who is an association official is relatively free to act without consultation with his organization, especially if he is very experienced in lobbying. For example, a lobbyist who is also vice-president of his association reports:

> I would probably make the initial judgments . . . because of my particular role in the association and because of the fact that I have had considerable experience in the legislature. I pretty much know what position the association can be expected to take. On major bills there are occasions when I might have a skull session with the other officers, but as a rule I set the standard.

The lobbyist who offered these comments identifies strongly with the lobbying occupation but at the same time identifies with the goals of his association.

Nevertheless, there is still the possibility of organizational commitment exceeding commitment to the occupation. We will have occasion to comment upon this possibility further when we examine the extent to which lobbyists have an occupational identification. We would suspect, for example, that occupational identification is difficult to achieve in Utah because of the great personal commitment that lobbyists in that state have to their organizations. We also noted in the preceding chapter that there are fewer lawyers in Utah than in any other state. Since the model of collegial relationships is that of the legal profession, it is significant that in every state lobbyists who were trained in law hold less of a personal interest in the organization they represent than do members of other occupational groups (Table 4.4). It may be that the ideal of

TABLE 4.4

Percentages of Lawyers and Non-Lawyers Who Feel
a Personal Interest in Goals of the Organization

	Lawyers	(N)	Non-Lawyers	(N)
Massachusetts	51%	(52)	62%	(133)
North Carolina	41	(71)	55	(61)
Oregon	45	(56)	59	(137)
Utah	43	(29)	75	(104)

the lawyer who represents his client with objectivity carries over into the relationship between the lawyer-lobbyist and his organization client.

Identification with the Role of Lobbyist

Competing with the organization for the loyalty of the lobbyist is the occupation. Loyalty to an occupation is predicated on feeling a sense of belonging to the occupation. One might suspect that such a sense of belonging is difficult, if not impossible, for lobbyists to achieve, since their job entails competition among themselves; but such is not the case. In North Carolina and Utah, a substantial minority of lobbyists feel a sense of belonging to the lobbying profession; in Massachusetts, a clear majority feel this sense of belonging; in Oregon, two thirds of the lobbyists feel it (see Table 4.5).

TABLE 4.5

Percentage of Lobbyists with a Sense of Belonging to Lobbying Profession

		(N)
Massachusetts	56%	(185)
North Carolina	48	(132)
Oregon	67	(193)
Utah	41	(134)

The unusually high percentage of Oregon lobbyists who feel a sense of identification with their occupation is probably related to the existence in that state of a formal association of lobbyists, the Capitol Club. Eighteen percent of the Oregon lobbyists who have a feeling of identification indicate that the reason for this feeling is that they meet regularly with other lobbyists. Substantially fewer of the lobbyists in other states offer this reason. Oregon lobbyists are also more likely to indicate that they have a fraternal feeling for one another, and less likely to state that only lobbyists with similar interests have a sense of identification. In no other state have lobbyists so systematically institutionalized their relationships. The Capitol Club originated because of a legislative effort to impose stricter regulations upon lobbyists. There had been occasions when the behavior of lobbyists had incensed legislators, causing them to institute legislation calling for the reporting by lobbyists of their expenditures. Lobbyists organized themselves for the purpose of preventing the passage of such legislation by instituting self-imposed rules of conduct. From that base, the organization developed into a medium for increased interaction among lobbyists. As one lobbyist put it:

> It's an opportunity to identify officially with an organization and it also provides an opportunity for lobbyists to get together and discuss some of our problems. We kind of share one another's problems and I think it provides us with an opportunity to get out and meet some other lobbyists with whom we would ordinarily not meet.

But the Capitol Club has gone beyond the simple function of facilitating contact among lobbyists; it now also contributes to the development of fraternal feelings among lobbyists:

> One specific instance that I can recall is when one lobbyist had a very unfortunate illness, so we called a meeting of the Capitol Club and discussed it among ourselves. He was one of the boys so we just recommended that we quietly raise the money.

The case of the Capitol Club points to an important distinction to be made between the identification of Oregon lobbyists and the identification of, for example, Massachusetts lobbyists. In Oregon, interaction between lobbyists is not restricted to lobbyists of the same ideological persuasion. In Massachusetts, on the other hand, interaction is governed to some extent by common ideological goals. Therefore, while the identification of the Oregon lobbyist is with his occupation as a whole, the identification of the Massachusetts lobbyist is with an occupational subgroup, a subgroup consisting of only those lobbyists who share a common ideological commitment. The basic loyalty of the Massachusetts lobbyist is to his group, rather than to his occupation. His identification with his organization inhibits his development of reciprocal relations with colleagues. It is probable that in Oregon the existence of a formal organization has to some extent muted the antagonisms that one lobbyist might have for another who represents an opposing interest. In this context, identification with the profession has been allowed to occur through a process (similar to Truman's concept of overlapping membership) in which lobbyists expand their reference group to include their colleagues.

The notion of the expansion of the reference group of lobbyists can be further illustrated by the fact that 42 percent of Oregon lobbyists say they communicate frequently with lobbyists who represent interests opposed to their own (see Table 4.6). This is almost twice as many as in the next closest state, North Carolina, and almost four times as many as in Massachusetts. The interchange

TABLE 4.6

Percentage of Lobbyists Who
Have Frequent Communication
with Opposition Lobbyists

		(N)
Massachusetts	11%	(185)
North Carolina	25	(132)
Oregon	42	(193)
Utah	20	(134)

between lobbyists in Oregon, therefore, is closer to the interaction between lawyers than the interactions between lobbyists in other states. Oregon lobbyists are capable of putting aside their ideological antagonisms and interacting on a professional basis. Oregon "regulars" frequently point out that, while they are forced to oppose other lobbyists, they still find them to be congenial people. In fact, some Oregon lobbyists prefer to interact with the "regulars" who are their opponents in contrast to those who, while in ideological agreement, are not part of the inner circle. For instance, a lobbyist was asked about his relations with another lobbyist with whom he shared similar legislative interests. He replied, "_____ is one lobbyist I don't hold in the same high regard that I do most of the others." The reason for this negative evaluation was related entirely to the tactics employed by the other lobbyist. "He threatens legislators in a number of different ways and puts on the pressure campaign. He is overbearing in his attitude toward legislators." On the other hand, the lobbyist spoke of one of his colleagues with whom he is frequently in disagreement in the following manner: "I am very good friends with him. We contest an issue. Maybe he will win, but that is the way the game is played. He works for an organization that I have to oppose but we both recognize that we do the best we can to win our point." In other words, the issue to be contested is less important than the display of proper form.

There are, however, even in Oregon, large numbers of lobbyists who do not feel a sense of belonging to the lobbying profession. In many cases, especially in Oregon, those lobbyists who fail to achieve a sense of professional identification are those who are not really very active practitioners of their trade. One must be an active lobbyist to be part of the "ingroup." "One-shot" lobbyists, whose appearances at the legislature are sporadic, are not likely to penetrate to the inner circle. Hence, in Oregon, beginners feel that there is not yet a place for them in the Capitol Club. The beginning lobbyist undergoes a "hazing" process prior to full acceptance. Consider, for example, the testimony of one lobbyist who later became an officer of the Capitol Club:

> My first session was in 1955. It seemed to me then that lobbyists formed a very exclusive club. I was new to the legislature and new to the state and nobody knew me. I spent three days looking for a floor pass, which, of course, isn't required. It was like the old business of snipe hunting. I don't know when the magic time came but all of a sudden I was a lobbyist with a capital L. Things started to fall into line for me by the end of the first session. I was not yet accepted as a regular, but they knew that I would be back. Other lobbyists began to be helpful in pointing me in the right direction. The grapevine began to be useful to me.

One advantage accruing from acceptance by colleagues, then, is immediate and tangible: information becomes easier to gather.

The Ethics of Lobbying

Lobbyists do not have the formal code of ethics characteristic of professions, but they have developed an informal code of ethics, a set of unwritten, subtly enforced standards of behavior. Except in Utah, a substantial majority of lobbyists indicate an awareness of such a code (Table 4.7). Interestingly, an overwhelming majority of legislators in all four states believe that a code of ethics for lobbyists exists. It is curious that legislators should be more likely to believe this than lobbyists themselves. However, their greater awareness of a code of ethics might in part be a consequence of the fact that they interact much more with full-time lobbyists than with part-time lobbyists. Furthermore, since our sample of lobbyists includes a majority of part-time people, we would expect the per-

ception of a code of ethics to be lower than it would be if that
sample consisted entirely of full-time people. Since the code of
ethics is informal, full-time lobbyists are more likely than part-time
lobbyists to be aware of its existence and to participate in it consistently. Given the discrepancy between the estimates of legislators
and lobbyists, it is nevertheless true that each estimate corresponds

TABLE 4.7

Percentages of Legislators and
Lobbyists Aware of a Code of Ethics

	Legislators	(N)	Lobbyists	(N)
Massachusetts	75%	(224)	58%	(185)
North Carolina	74	(164)	58	(132)
Oregon	92	(84)	75	(193)
Utah	62	(90)	43	(134)

roughly with the other. Thus, for example, the highest percentage
of both legislators and lobbyists aware of a code of ethics occurs in
Oregon and the lowest percentage of both groups aware of a code
occurs in Utah.

The question of the extent to which a code of ethics is actually
operative is distinct from the question of whether or not a code
exists. If there are rules of conduct but no feeling of necessity to
follow them, a code would be totally ineffective. However, of those
legislators and lobbyists who believe that a code of ethics exists, the
inclination is to think that it is applied consistently (see Table 4.8).

TABLE 4.8

Percentages of Legislators and Lobbyists Believing
Code of Ethics is Applied "All" or "Most" of the Time

	Legislators	(N)*	Lobbyists	(N)
Massachusetts	69%	(182)	59%	(108)
North Carolina	73	(121)	80	(76)
Oregon	96	(77)	86	(145)
Utah	75	(56)	65	(57)

* N = those who believe a code of ethics exists.

Oregon, the state with the highest percentage of legislators and lobbyists who believe that a code exists, is also the state with the highest percentage of both groups of respondents who believe that the code is applied frequently. The heavy commitment of the Oregon respondents to a code of ethics may be partially attributable to the existence in that state of a formal organization, an organization whose practices probably tend to make the existence of a code more obvious. A former president of the Capitol Club, asked if the association actually polices lobbyists, replied:

> You're darn right we do. If anybody interrupts me, for example, I have a little piece of his arm right in my teeth. I happen to be an officer of the Capitol Club this year and if some guy is misbehaving we'll have a meeting and ask the fellow to lay off. If we don't get any reaction from the fellow, then we get various members of the legislature, mainly the leaders, to help us out. The next thing you know, the guy will be badgered to death in the next hearing he shows up at. Or he may have a difficult time even getting an opportunity to testify.

Thus, not only do these lobbyists enforce a code of ethics, but they are able to utilize legislators in enforcing the code. Even in a state without a formal organization, legislators may in some way be made a part of the enforcement process. A Massachusetts lobbyist described an enforcement procedure used against violators of the code of ethics in his state:

> There is a little undercurrent of knifing that can go on. Adverse reports about the lobbyist would circulate among the members of the legislature. We would see to that. . . . If there is something adverse about a character that he wishes would not be spread around, you just put it on the grapevine and spread it and that does its evil work.

Notice, however, that the Massachusetts lobbyist does not specifically indicate any penalty other than the placing of the lobbyist in a bad light before legislators.

The particulars of the code of ethics vary somewhat from state to state. Our depth interviews indicated that lobbyists in Oregon are especially concerned about their colleagues visibly badgering legislators. In other states, such as Massachusetts, the utilization of "pressure tactics" is a more accepted part of the lobbying process and is not considered a violation. However, there are certain fundamental rules which seem to apply in every state. These rules apply to relations between lobbyists more directly than to relations between lobbyists and legislators. One of the basic rules is never to interrupt a lobbyist who is talking to a legislator. This is a serious offense, since much of the time of the lobbyist is spent "hanging around" waiting to get the ear of a busy legislator. Given the press of time, they are especially anxious to avoid distraction when they are talking to legislators. The second rule is to avoid attacking the position of another lobbyist unless it is necessary in defense of one's own point of view. Most lobbyists will not involve themselves in a struggle which does not concern them directly, even if requested to do so by legislators. If a legislator asks a lobbyist to help him out, the lobbyist will normally find out if there are any other lobbyists who would oppose his intervention. If there are, he will avoid getting involved; if there are not, involvement is acceptable. A lobbyist explained this:

> Many times legislators come to you and ask for help, which I will do providing that I am not encroaching on some other lobbyist's territory. In other words, there is a code of ethics among lobbyists; you can't try to beat another lobbyist unless you have some real reason for doing so. When a legislator asks me to give him a little help on a bill, as long as it is not an important bill of another lobbyist, I would do it.

The sanctions against violations of the rules in no way approximate the formality of, for example, a disbarment procedure. Nor can lobbyists control entry into the occupation. However, as we have seen, it is possible for lobbyists to enforce a code of ethics informally. Thus, by the criteria listed earlier in this chapter, the job of the lobbyist does not fall at the extreme "unprofessional" end of the continuum. Informally, "rites of passage" are established, rules of conduct are developed, and sanctions are imposed.

It is important to realize, however, that because lobbyists have no access to formal sanctions, the extent to which codes of ethics can be enforced depends to some extent upon the commitment of lobbyists to the occupation. We shall have occasion to return to the topic of commitment later in the chapter. For the moment, it is useful to observe that lobbyists who take their job more seriously are more likely to be concerned about incurring sanctions. These are usually active lobbyists, and active lobbyists are those against whom sanctions are most frequently imposed. Outsiders, those who are rarely seen at the legislature, are generally treated with more tolerance. An outsider is not expected to be fully cognizant of the norms of behavior. Thus, when speaking of rules of conduct, lobbyists frequently qualify their statements with such comments as, "I am speaking now only of the full-time people. Anyone who wants to can lobby, has a perfect right to do it, and we treat them with understanding. We wouldn't do the things to them that we do to each other and we overlook a lot of things they do." Only about 25 percent of lobbyists, however, are "full-time"—that is, committed to lobbying as a career.

Occupational Socialization

As is true of any occupation, lobbyists go through a period of socialization during which they develop necessary skills and commitment to the occupation. In many occupations, some of this socialization takes place during a period of formal training, but, since lobbyists receive no formal training, all of their socialization must be of the on-the-job variety.

Prior to his actual arrival at the legislature, the lobbyist has no way to learn the rules of the game or the code of ethics which lobbyists maintain governs their behavior. Once he has arrived, the rate at which he is likely to learn the rules varies from state to state. In Oregon, a state with a high rate of intra-occupational interaction, the young lobbyist will probably have the opportunity to receive explicit instruction from more experienced lobbyists. A veteran Oregon lobbyist described the process:

> In 1947, when I first came down here, I was 29 years old and nobody would even talk to me. That's all changed now. When a youngster comes down the other fellows help him. You just start out and you listen and you watch and you counsel those people who will counsel with you, and if you got any brains at all, it doesn't take long to find out that you've got to know the ground rules.

In states without high rates of intra-occupational interaction, lobbyists appear to go through a longer period of socialization. It takes longer for them to become aware of and to accept the norms of the occupation. Thus, while in all states veteran lobbyists are more likely than novices to feel a sense of belonging to the lobbying profession, in Oregon the difference in identification between novices and veterans is minimal (see Table 4.9). Freshmen there quickly get a good idea of what is expected of them.

TABLE 4.9

Percentage of Lobbyists with a Sense of Belonging
to Lobbying Profession, by Experience

	EXPERIENCE					
	Low (0–2 years)	(N)	Medium (3–10 years)	(N)	High (11 years or more)	(N)
Massachusetts	43%	(37)	52%	(93)	70%	(59)
North Carolina	30	(20)	51	(43)	50	(68)
Oregon	62	(58)	69	(71)	68	(56)
Utah	25	(16)	47	(59)	40	(58)

The Extent of Commitment

Although there is a relationship between occupational socialization and length of time on the job, the relationship is not simple. Many lobbyists who have been involved in the occupation for a number of years are actually amateur lobbyists—that is to say, they customarily show up at a legislative session only once or twice to present testimony at a formal hearing. The committed lobbyist, even if he has been involved in lobbying for fewer years, is likely to spend a great deal more time at the legislature than the uncommitted lobbyist. In order to measure more precisely the extent of commitment to the occupation, an index of job investment was constructed. Our interviews revealed that lobbyists themselves judge whether or not a colleague qualifies as a full-time lobbyist on the basis of three factors: (1) the number of years he has been involved in lobbying, (2) the number of hours per day he devotes to the job, and (3) the number of interactions he has with legislators. Clearly, an index built on these three components is not a perfect measure of commitment. Nonetheless, it does give us some idea of the proportion of lobbyists who are deeply involved in the occupation. As Table 4.10 indicates, a minority of lobbyists have invested heavily in their jobs.[4] In Massachusetts commitment to the job is minimal; even in Oregon, where conditions for commitment are more favorable, only 30 percent of lobbyists are high investors. In general, these figures confirm the impressionistic estimates of lobbyists.

TABLE 4.10

Job Investment of Lobbyists

	Low	Medium	High	(N)
Massachusetts	45%	49	5	(185)
North Carolina	20%	57	24	(132)
Oregon	21%	50	30	(193)
Utah	24%	56	20	(134)

Lobbyists in Oregon, however, interact with legislators at a higher rate than lobbyists in other states and spend more hours per day on the job (a mean of 7.7 hours per day, as compared to 2.5 hours for lobbyists in Massachusetts, 3.9 for lobbyists in North Carolina, and 4.5 for lobbyists in Utah). Thus, Oregon lobbyists would clearly rank higher in commitment were it not for the fact that they are more mobile than lobbyists in other states. This is further evidence that the number of years one has been a lobbyist is not in itself a measure of his commitment. Relative ease of movement, a factor usually associated with problems of supply and demand, is a variable which intervenes in the simple relationship between commitment and longevity. In Oregon, lobbyists are held in relatively high repute by both legislators and administrators. For this reason, they are more likely than lobbyists in other states to find it possible to move on to more attractive jobs. The president of the Capitol Club recalled with pride that "The lobbyists in this state have gone some place." He then mentioned several ex-lobbyists who became Congressmen.

As we would expect, lobbyists who have invested highly are much more likely to have a sense of belonging to the lobbying profession than those who are low investors (see Table 4.11). In every state, more high-investment lobbyists than low-investment lobbyists have a

---

[4] Patterson (see note 2), using an index based upon amount of time lobbying, occupation, and percentage of income derived from lobbying, found 40 percent of Illinois lobbyists to be "professional."

TABLE 4.11

Percentage of Lobbyists with a Sense of Belonging
to Lobbying Profession, by Job Investment

	Low	(N)	Medium	(N)	High	(N)
Massachusetts	48%	(84)	59%	(90)	91%	(11)
North Carolina	42	(26)	48	(75)	52	(31)
Oregon	48	(40)	69	(96)	77	(57)
Utah	34	(32)	40	(75)	52	(27)

sense of belonging. Identification and investment develop together.
Thus, in lobbying, as in other occupations, there is an ingroup.

The Work of the Lobbyist

As we mentioned above, one measure of job investment is the
extent of a lobbyist's interaction with legislators. However, the job
of the lobbyist entails a variety of tasks, such as administrative
work and the preparation of information requested by legislators,
not directly related to personal contact with legislators. Patterson,
in studying the lobbyists of Oklahoma, found three distinct role
orientations. First, there is the *contact man*, who "conceives of his
job as primarily that of making contacts, personal acquaint-
anceships, and friendships with individual legislators." Next, there
is the *informant*, who prepares information for distribution to legislators in order to present his client's case in the most effective
manner. Finally, there is the *watchdog*, who devotes his time to
scrutinizing the legislative calendar in order to alert his client
organization about various bills that might affect it.[5]

In this section we will estimate the proportion of their time that
lobbyists assign to various activities, using Patterson's categorization (with some modification).as a guide. Our estimates are based
on a description by lobbyists of how they spend an average day. The
following is an example of such a description:

> I will get down to the capitol regularly at seven fifteen or
> seven thirty in the morning and will have breakfast in the capitol
> coffeeshop. There will usually be some legislators there and I

[5] Patterson, p. 83.

will sit with them and we will talk. Quite often they will be
members of one of my committees that will meet at eight o'clock.
I will go to the committee meetings whether or not I testify. I
cover all the committee hearings as far as I can to be able to
answer questions. That period will be over about nine thirty and
we'll go back to the coffeeshop with a different group of people
and sit down with them. They will go upstairs at ten o'clock to
sit through the session. I will go upstairs and call the office, talk
to some other lobbyists and go down and have another cup of
coffee with some other lobbyists. We will compare notes. The
session adjourns at a quarter to twelve. I will pick up a couple
of legislators and take them out to lunch in the coffeeshop or
somewhere else.

Quite often I will have a one o'clock hearing. If not, by this
time the doors to the floor are open. Let us assume that it is still
early in the session and they aren't meeting afternoons. I will
talk to many legislators on the floor, stand around and wait for
them, quite often because they are being called to the phone or
someone else is talking to them, and you line up back there and
it looks like a bull ring or something. I also will check with
committee clerks somewhere in this interim. We will read the bills
that were introduced or printed the day before. You will pick up
those that apply to you. If you have time, then you will start
doing some research or I will go down to the three o'clock hearing
if there is one. If not, then I will spend my time on the floor of
the Senate or the House.

Five o'clock or five thirty you will leave. I will go up to the
apartment, sit down and have a drink, and, if I am taking someone out to dinner I get dressed for dinner and we go out. If not,
we run what we call the track-line, which is running the bars to
see who is out with whom. Quite often there is a legislator out by
himself. You see who is with whom. Notice how the alliances are
building up. About midnight or one o'clock I call it a day and go
home.

It is apparent that this lobbyist is more of a contact man than an
informant. His remarks also illustrate how much of the lobbyist's
time is consumed by "hurrying up to wait." Lobbying is likely to
take fifteen or more hours per day if conducted in the above
fashion. We can divide this time into two general categories. The
first of these is administrative time, which is spent by the lobbyist in
his office doing substantive research, or preparing testimony or
speeches, or writing letters. This category is similar to Patterson's
informant and watchdog categories. The second major division is
time devoted to contact or attempts at contact within the legislative
arena itself. This includes time spent with members of the legisla-

ture, time spent with other persons dealing with subjects related to legislative work, and time spent simply hanging around waiting for something to happen. This type of activity is characteristic of Patterson's contact man.

We are drawing a distinction between time allocated to interaction and time allocated to administrative efforts. These two types of activities occupy most of the time of the lobbyist. As Table 4.12

TABLE 4.12

Percentage of Lobbyists Categorized as Contact Men or Administrators

	Massachusetts	North Carolina	Oregon	Utah
Administrators	61%	48%	36%	48%
Contact Men	30	39	54	46
Equally Both	9	12	10	7
(N)	(185)	(132)	(193)	(134)

indicates, lobbyists, except in Oregon, actually spend more of their time in administrative chores than in contact work. Indeed, in Massachusetts and North Carolina administrative work clearly dominates. In Utah and Oregon substantially more contact work is undertaken. Patterson has noted that a greater amount of contact work is typical of full-time lobbyists. Our data supports this conclusion. In every state, the more time a lobbyist invests in the job, the lower is the percentage of time he devotes to administrative details and the greater is the percentage of time he spends in contact with other people (see Table 4.13). We can carry the argument further by noting that those who identify with the lobbying profession spend much more of their time in contact work and tend to avoid administrative work. Hence, those lobbyists who participate directly in the legislative process, those who are making more contacts with legislators, are those who have a strong sense of belonging to the lobbying profession. The professional lobbyist is one who conceives of his job as contacting other people. The more he has invested in his job, the greater is the amount of time he spends in contact work. As the lobbyist quoted above said, "If you have time, you do some research." Legislators, as we shall see, want information from lobbyists. Lobbyists, however, believe that research and

information are not enough. Success requires the personal touch.
Thus, "contact men" and "professional lobbyists" become synony-
mous terms.

TABLE 4.13

Percentage of Lobbyists Categorized as Contact
Men or Administrators, by Job Investment

	Massachusetts	North Carolina	Oregon	Utah
LOW INVESTORS				
Administrators	68%	54%	48%	66%
Contact Men	26	42	33	22
Equally Both	6	4	20	13
(N)	(84)	(26)	(40)	(32)
MEDIUM INVESTORS				
Aministrators	58%	52%	38%	44%
Contact Men	30	31	54	49
Equally Both	12	17	10	7
(N)	(90)	(75)	(96)	(75)
HIGH INVESTORS				
Administrators	27%	35%	28%	37%
Contact Men	64	58	70	63
Equally Both	9	6	2	8
(N)	(11)	(31)	(57)	(27)

5 HOW LEGISLATORS AND LOBBYISTS INTERACT

An analysis of an interaction begins with a description of the images of self and others held by the participants in the interaction. In the previous chapter, we concentrated upon the lobbyist's self-perception. It is now appropriate to supplement these lobbyist self-images with the self-images of legislators and with legislators' images of the lobbyist, and to explore the interweaving of these images in the process of interaction.

One person's image of another can refer both to a generalized sentiment and to a specific picture of the characteristics of the other. Generalized attitudes toward a significant other can be phrased simply in terms of positive and negative impressions, although these impressions are productive of more specific and articulate judgments. The relationship between generalized sentiment and interaction is direct: If persons like each other they will interact; if they dislike each other they will cease the interaction.[1] Interaction, therefore, should be clearly predicted by sentiment. Sentiment, in turn, is largely a function of attitude similarity. In sum, those people who have similar values tend to like one another and to interact on the basis of this generalized positive sentiment.[2]

[1] See George C. Homans, *The Human Group* (New York: Harcourt, Brace & World, 1950), p. 112.

[2] For an experimental illustration of this relationship, see Theodore M. Newcomb, ''The Prediction of Interpersonal Attraction,'' *American Psychologist*, 11 (1956), 575–586. In Newcomb's experiment, strangers were measured with regard to attitude similarity prior to meeting one another. They were then placed in a college rooming

The relationship between sentiment and interaction described above is, of course, based on the assumption that each actor is free to accept or reject the other as a partner in the interaction. In the legislator-lobbyist interaction, however, one partner, at least formally, has greater freedom than the other. The legislator has the power to vote; the lobbyist has an interest in that vote. Therefore, the lobbyist must seek to interact. Since the lobbyist has no formal power but is dependent upon one who does, interaction is a matter of necessity for him.

If the legislator-lobbyist relationship is not as free of constraint as in the typical experimental situation, does the experimentally derived hypothesis still work? Table 5.1, compiled from data from all four states of our study, indicates that it does. In this table, an index of interaction based upon a series of questions measuring the frequency of a variety of types of contacts is run against a scale measuring general attitudes of legislators toward lobbyists. The data reveal that attitude and frequency of interaction are positively related.[3] The element of constraint in this special case of interac-

TABLE 5.1

Legislators' Interaction and Attitude toward Lobbyists

Attitude toward Lobbyists		Rate of Interaction	
	Low	Medium	High
Negative	52%	30%	11%
Neutral	37	36	27
Positive	11	34	61
	100%	100%	99%*
(N)	(191)	(197)	(174)

* Percentage does not equal 100 due to rounding.

tion, in other words, does not produce a deviation from the theoretical model of interaction. Legislators are more likely to accept interaction with lobbyists toward whom they have a more favorable attitude.

---

house in pairs unrelated to attitudes. In spite of the creation of a natural interaction situation in terms of physical proximity, individuals who were most similar to one another were most likely to interact.

[3] Of course, one might just as easily argue that interaction is a *cause* of positive attitude. Indeed, the American spirit of compromise implies that if people can just ''get together'' they can work out solutions to their problems.

Given, then, that the generalized attitude of legislators toward lobbyists can be relied upon as a predictor of interaction, what specific judgments of lobbyists by legislators are most crucial in encouraging or discouraging interaction? In order to obtain such judgments, we asked both legislators and lobbyists to indicate traits which they believe characterize lobbyists as a group. No restrictions were imposed upon the respondents. They were not required to check off appropriate adjectives from a list supplied by the interviewer but were free to volunteer any comments they wished. This resulted in a variety of response categories, but four characteristics were mentioned far more frequently than any others and will be used in this analysis. They are (1) good personality, (2) intelligence and knowledgeability, (3) aggressiveness, and (4) honesty. In Table 5.2, the perceptions of legislators and lobbyists are arranged by state and by frequency of interaction. The table thus makes possible three levels of analysis: (1) by legislative role, (2) by level of interaction, and (3) by state.

In examining differences in perception by legislative role, we will base our comments primarily upon the high-interaction category. Such an examination reveals that, except in Utah, more legislators than lobbyists have images of lobbyists as possessing a pleasing and facilitating personality and as being intelligent and knowledgeable. On the other hand, more lobbyists than legislators think of lobbyists as aggressive. In spite of the fact that both groups tend to think more in terms of personality than any other characteristic, we can make the generalization that legislators tend to emphasize the pleasing and facilitating aspects of the lobbyist image, while lobbyists themselves emphasize the persuasive or technique-oriented aspects of their image. Lobbyists are more likely to see themselves as effective salesmen who possess persuasive skills. Legislators, on the other hand, do not like to think of themselves as subject to manipulation by either pure charm or aggressiveness; rather, they like to think of themselves as being impressed by reason and intelligence.

With respect to honesty, no clear pattern for all four states can be discerned. In North Carolina and Utah, more lobbyists than legislators perceive lobbyists as a group as essentially honest; in Massachusetts and Oregon, the reverse is true. Indeed, it is striking that none of the highly active Massachusetts lobbyists choose to describe themselves as honest.

Turning to a consideration of the relation between the lobbyist's image and the rate of interaction, we note that in general (in states

TABLE 5.2

Perceived Characteristics of Lobbyists, by State, Rate of Interaction, and Occupation

RATE OF INTERACTION

Perception of Lobbyists	Massachusetts				North Carolina				Oregon				Utah			
	Low	Me-dium	High	Aver-age	Low	Me-dium	High	Aver-age	Low*	Me-dium	High	Aver-age	Low*	Me-dium	High	Aver-age
LEGISLATORS																
Good personality	36%**	39%	37%	37%	62%	57%	46%	59%		56%	52%	52%		22%	42%	38%
Intelligent and knowledgeable	28	47	50	38	35	53	49	45		31	44	38		22	27	24
Aggressive	15	18	24	17	21	11	14	18		16	10	13		15	20	17
Honest	8	15	17	11	10	12	6	10		16	38	29		4	13	9
(N)	(121)	(85)	(38)		(71)	(50)	(35)		(4)	(32)	(48)		(8)	(27)	(35)	
LOBBYISTS																
Good personality	25	44	33	25	29	57	67	54	28	25	44	38	21	41	45	38
Intelligent and knowledgeable	24	44	47	32	10	20	36	23	28	34	30	31	14	24	34	26
Aggressive	24	13	37	23	23	16	16	17	18	13	17	16	14	26	21	22
Honest	4	15	0	6	3	11	27	14	10	14	29	20	4	10	32	18
(N)	(116)	(39)	(30)		(31)	(56)	(45)		(39)	(71)	(83)		(28)	(50)	(56)	

* Too few cases for computation of percentages.

** Total percentages may exceed 100 because of multiple responses.

where low interaction is discernible) the legislator's tendency to think of lobbyists in terms of personality decreases as interaction increases, but that the lobbyist's tendency to think of himself in terms of personality increases as interaction increases. In a sense, then, general personality images begin as stereotypic for legislators and are replaced by more explicit images as relationships develop. Lobbyists, however, as we would expect, do not view themselves as a group in terms of stereotypes. As a relationship develops, the characteristic of intelligence and knowledgeability is the one most likely to replace personality as the predominant element in the lobbyist's image. The tendency of both groups to think of lobbyists in terms of this characteristic increases as interaction increases.

Judgments concerning aggressiveness reflect state patterns more than interaction patterns. In North Carolina the pattern is unclear, but in Massachusetts and Utah, the more often a legislator interacts with lobbyists the more aggressive lobbyists seem to him, while in Oregon the pattern is exactly the reverse. A similarly conflicting pattern develops for the characteristic of honesty. In general, except in North Carolina, more high-interaction legislators select this characteristic than do low-interaction legislators; except in Massachusetts, the same is true for lobbyists.

In spite of these numerous qualifications and exceptions, rate of interaction does seem to have a significant effect on the lobbyist's image. In view of the differing responses of legislators and lobbyists, it is difficult to generalize about the relation of state to image. However, one can observe that the characteristic of personality is most typical of responses in North Carolina and least typical of responses in Massachusetts and Utah. The characteristic of intelligence and knowledgeability is fairly evenly distributed in all states except Utah. Perceptions in terms of aggressive behavior are typical of Massachusetts and Utah and very atypical of Oregon. Finally, Oregon and Massachusetts stand at opposite ends of a continuum for the characteristic of honesty. Relating these patterns to the effectiveness of lobbyists, we note that the two characteristics which seem to distinguish Oregon, the state with the strongest lobbies, are perceptions of honesty and perceptions of the absence of aggressiveness. It is sometimes assumed that the basic resource of the lobbyist is the possession of technical information unavailable to the poorly staffed state legislator, but the importance given to the characteristic of knowledgeability is typical of weak-lobby as well as strong-lobby states. It may be speculated, therefore, that the basic resource at the disposal of a lobbyist is actually the creation in the mind of the legislator of the image of honesty and the avoidance of the image of aggressiveness. If we examine the high-interaction Oregon legislators, we note that they are more likely than the legislators of any other state to volunteer the comment that lobbyists are honest, but less likely to volunteer the comment that lobbyists are aggressive. On the other hand, the responses of the active Oregon legislators with regard to the intelligence of lobbyists do not differ markedly from those of the low-interaction legislators in weak-lobby states.

Images of Professionalism

The characteristics described above seem to be related to perceptions of ability. However, the relation is not complete; for example, legislators may believe lobbyists to be aggressive and not especially honest, but, at the same time, might consider them highly competent in the execution of their responsibilities. Whether a legislator would arrive at evaluations such as this would depend to some extent on the expectations attached to the political role of the lobbyist. If being aggressive and somewhat less than candid is an accepted mode of political activity, then lobbyists who do not project this sort of an image might be at a disadvantage. If, on the other hand, political activity is conceived of primarily in terms of integrity, lobbyists who are lacking in this characteristic presumably would be less effective. An evaluation of lobbying skills, therefore, must draw to some extent upon the nature of the expectations accruing to the political role of the lobbyist.

Seligman has suggested that a useful way to study occupational attitude on the political level is by means of the concept of *professionalism*.[4] Although generally applied primarily to legislators, this concept is equally applicable to lobbyists. Professionalism refers to a generalized body of skills possessed in common by members of a political elite. The acquisition of these skills is usually considered to be a function of experience. Thus, we talk about a seasoned politician as a ''professional'' and an inexperienced politician as an ''amateur.'' The professional is an expert in bargaining, a techni-

[4] Lester Seligman, ''The Professionalization of Political Elites: Toward an Occupational Analysis of the Legislator'' (unpublished manuscript, University of Oregon, 1964).

cian who can successfully control the amount, kind, and intensity of political conflict. Professionals are supposed to be sufficiently sophisticated in conflict management not to allow ideological disputes of the moment to become of primary importance. In Massachusetts, the slang word "pol" has been applied to this kind of politician.

The concept of professionalism also carries consequences for group cohesiveness. As a group of legislators or lobbyists increase in professionalism, they should increase their interaction and identification with colleagues. Colleagues become the primary reference group and a "fellowship of technicians" emerges. Identification with fellow professionals is expressed in conformity to the norms of colleagues, norms which compete in importance with the expectations of those outside the primary reference group. It follows that professionalism and cohesiveness should develop together and, further, that perceptions of professionalism should affect the influence of interest groups. Interest groups should be least effective in states where legislators are more professionally oriented, since for those legislators colleagues are the primary source of guidance.

To measure perceptions of professionalism, we use in our study an ordinally measured item stating, "The average legislator (lobbyist) is a competent professional who knows his business." Since this is a single item and not part of any scale, its validity is subject to the problem of response set. As a means of reducing the dangers of response set, we included another question concerned with perceptions of professionalism elsewhere in the interview schedule. The ordinally measured item and the other question indicate that the single item is reliable. Responses were rated on a six-point range of dispersion ranging from position one (strongly agree) to position six (strongly disagree). From the responses of each group (legislators and lobbyists in each state), a mean was computed as a way of providing a measure of the strength of each group's agreement with the interview statement, a mean of 1 indicating the strongest possible agreement. We took strength of agreement as an indication of how professional a group considered itself to be, of the extent or degree of professionalism members of the group felt the group as a whole to possess.

In order to explore the relationship between perceptions of professionalism and extent of cohesiveness, we decided to employ a measure of consensus. The greater the consensus among the members of the group—in other words, the greater the agreement among

TABLE 5.3

Perceptions of Professionalism of Legislators and Lobbyists, by State and Length of Service

Perception of Legislator as a Competent Professional

| | LENGTH OF SERVICE | | | |
	Low (2 years or less)	Medium (3–10 years)	High (11 years or More)	All
LEGISLATORS				
Massachusetts	.240* (2.42)**	.346 (2.28)	.319 (2.36)	.305 (2.32)
North Carolina	−.021 (3.31)	.251 (2.74)	.253 (2.88)	.150 (2.93)
Oregon	.059 (3.12)	.281 (2.82)	.333 (3.09)	.245 (2.94)
Utah	.175 (3.71)	.143 (3.57)	.333 (3.86)	.152 (3.66)
All	.119 (2.89)	.255 (2.85)	.310 (3.05)	.213 (2.96)
LOBBYISTS				
Massachusetts	.185 (2.89)	.297 (2.79)	.148 (3.24)	.229 (2.95)
North Carolina	.368 (2.74)	.085 (3.12)	.198 (2.83)	.181 (2.91)
Oregon	.158 (3.11)	.198 (3.19)	.157 (3.17)	.173 (3.13)
Utah	.297 (3.56)	.096 (3.70)	.046 (3.81)	.095 (3.73)
All	.251 (3.08)	.169 (3.20)	.136 (3.26)	.170 (3.18)

Perception of Lobbyist as a Competent Professional

| | LENGTH OF SERVICE | | | |
	Low (2 years or less)	Medium (3–10 years)	High (11 years or more)	All
LEGISLATORS				
Massachusetts	.473 (2.07)	.528 (1.71)	.615 (1.58)	.476 (1.80)
North Carolina	.431 (1.98)	.517 (2.01)	.847 (2.20)	.492 (2.03)
Oregon	.569 (2.18)	.647 (1.78)	.878 (1.73)	.658 (1.87)
Utah	.350 (2.56)	.366 (2.88)	.750 (1.88)	.380 (2.65)
All	.456 (2.20)	.515 (2.10)	.698 (1.85)	.501 (2.09)
LOBBYISTS				
Massachusetts	.477 (2.14)	.478 (2.13)	.497 (2.11)	.475 (2.12)
North Carolina	.467 (2.20)	.535 (2.14)	.590 (1.97)	.548 (2.07)
Oregon	.429 (2.34)	.517 (2.29)	.569 (2.06)	.494 (2.27)
Utah	.417 (2.38)	.264 (2.90)	.437 (2.64)	.354 (2.72)
All	.432 (2.27)	.449 (2.37)	.573 (2.20)	.468 (2.30)

* Consensus score.
** Mean response.

members of a group on a characteristic held in common—the greater the cohesiveness of the group. The measure of consensus we used was developed by Professor Robert K. Leik.[5] Leik's method measures the dispersion of answers. If all members of a group choose the same option, there is zero dispersion and perfect consensus. On the other hand, if the group divides into opposing factions of equal strength holding maximally divergent opinions, then the group shows zero consensus and maximum dispersion. The Leik index of consensus provides a theoretical range of -1.0 when 50 percent of responses are in each of the extreme categories, through 0.0 when responses are evenly divided among all categories, to $+1.0$ when all responses are in one category. In Table 5.3, consensus scores and mean responses to the interview item are tabulated by the length of time a lobbyist or legislator has served at his job. Length of service rather than rate of interaction is used here to test Seligman's suggestion that professionalization and development of cohesiveness are functions of career socialization. In any case, experience and interaction are closely related and can be counted the same for the purposes of this tabulation.

The table can be examined by comparing perceptions of self and other by legislative role, by state, and by experience. Each comparison provides certain distinct patterns. Comparing perceptions by legislative role, the following statements can be made. (1) Legislators see lobbyists as more professional than legislators themselves. (2) There is greater consensus among legislators about the professional skills of lobbyists than about their own skills. (3) Lobbyists see themselves as more professional than they see legislators. (4) There is greater consensus among lobbyists about their own professional skills than about the professional skills of legislators. Lobbyists, then, as seen by both groups, emerge as the professionals. Interestingly, however, the lobbyist's self-image is less professional than is the legislator's image of the lobbyist.

The extent to which these generalizations hold varies somewhat from state to state, and these variations suggest some quite significant conclusions about the effect of professionalism on interest-group influence. In looking at state-by-state patterns, it is helpful to use an aggregate index of professionalism compiled by merging the

[5] Robert K. Leik, "A Measure of Ordinal Consensus," *Pacific Sociological Review*, 9 (1966), 85–90. See also Michael A. Baer, "A Fortran Program for Computing the Leik Consensus Index 2," *Behavioral Science*, 12 (1967), 503.

views of both legislators and lobbyists (Table 5.4). These merged professionalism scores reveal that perceptions of professionalism are greatest in the states with the weakest lobbies and lowest in the states with the strongest lobbies. Furthermore, the discrepancy between legislators' perceptions of themselves and their perceptions of lobbyists is also greatest in the strong-lobby states. That is to say, legislators in Oregon and Utah see a greater discrepancy between their professional skills and lobbyists' professional skills than do legislators in Massachusetts and North Carolina. In Oregon and Utah there is a relative advantage to the lobbyist of 1.04, whereas the relative advantage to the lobbyist in the weak-lobby states is .67.

TABLE 5.4

Professionalism

	Mean
Massachusetts	2.26
North Carolina	2.48
Oregon	2.61
Utah	3.19

Seligman's suggestion is supported by these data. The development of professionalism does contribute to group cohesiveness and to a concomitant decline in the influence of "outsiders." In this case, the outsiders happen to be interest groups. In states in which legislators lack a strong sense of professionalism, the development of close ingroup feelings is not likely to occur. As a result, the institutional structure of those states is more open and, therefore, easier for lobbyists to penetrate. Even within a relatively closed institutional structure, however, those individual legislators whose self-image is less professional than the self-images of their colleagues are more likely to be influenced by lobbyists.

Schlesinger has related professionalism to opportunity structure. He notes that the fewer the political opportunities in a state, the more likely it is that the state's political leaders will have made an early start on their careers. He equates an early start in politics with a strong career orientation. Hence, closed opportunity structures contribute to the professional orientations of politicians. In corroboration of the evidence presented here, Schlesinger ranks the opportunity structures of Utah and Oregon as more open than those of Massachusetts and North Carolina.[6]

Within the opportunity structure of a state, the legislature is likely to provide the greatest opportunity for political life and also to be the most transitional of public offices. This means that in a state legislature stable interaction patterns cannot be fully developed and that a state legislator has a difficult time developing a professional self-image. The legislators in the four states under consideration here have been on the job for an average of only six years. Hence it is not surprising that the consensus of these legislators about the lobbying role is generally higher than their consensus about their own role. More particularly, variations among the states of our study seem to confirm a relation between opportunity structure, professionalism, and strength of interest groups. Utah, for example, exhibits very low consensus and very low conception of professional status. The opportunity structure in Utah is substantially more open than that of any other state and the mean experience of Utah legislators is substantially less than in any other state. Utah, finally, as we have said before, is a strong-lobby state.

The third way of examining the table, in terms of career patterns, provides evidence that stability of interaction contributes to consensus but not to perceptions of professionalism. The following statements clarify this general conclusion: (1) As legislators become more experienced, their consensus about their own professional skills increases, but their perceptions of the *extent* of their professional skills does not change very much. In fact, it remains the same in Oregon and actually decreases in Utah. (2) Among lobbyists, in contrast, both consensus and perception of degree of professional skills increase as stability of interaction increases. (3) As legislators' perception of their own skills declines, their perception of lobbyists' skills tends to increase. (4) As the consensus of lobbyists about the skills of legislators decreases, the consensus of lobbyists about their own skills increases. (5) As the perceptions of lobbyists of the extent of skills among legislators decreases, their perception of the extent of their own skills increases. In short, despite the fact that the legislature is a formal institution and that lobbyists, for the most part, are not formally organized (the exception is Oregon), the relationship between length of time in the occupation and both consensus and professionalism is substantially clearer for lobbyists.

[6] Joseph A. Schlesinger, *Ambition and Politics* (Chicago: Rand McNally & Co., 1966), pp. 51, 100.

The transitory nature of the legislative office, in contrast to the more permanent nature of the lobbying occupation, seems a feasible explanation for this occurrence. These data describe patterns of belief with respect to the existence of professionalism, but say nothing about the existence of professionalism itself. It may well be that the achieving of professional status is not necessarily desirable in states where the norms are oriented toward amateurism. That is to say, if the political climate of a state is such that "professional" means something roughly akin to "party hack" or, in the case of lobbyists, refers to one whose manipulative skills render his sincerity suspect, the possession of a professional image might be a disadvantage. Since we have characterized Oregon and Utah as amateur states and Massachusetts and North Carolina as professional states, we would expect perceptions of professionalism to relate negatively to attitude in the former pair of states and positively to attitude in the latter pair of states. Indeed, in Massachusetts, as attitude toward lobbyists becomes more favorable, perceptions of the lobbyists as professionals increase; in Utah, the reverse is true: the more favorable the attitude, the less professional the image of the lobbyist (see Table 5.5). In Oregon, however, there is no clear pattern, and the pattern

TABLE 5.5

Perceptions of Professionalism and Legislators' Attitude toward Lobbyists

| | ATTITUDE | | |
	Negative	Neutral	Positive
Massachusetts	.416* (2.00)**	.531 (1.82)	.677 (1.48)
North Carolina	.517 (1.94)	.492 (2.09)	.458 (2.13)
Oregon	.733 (1.40)	.700 (2.05)	.654 (1.86)
Utah	.531 (1.86)	.455 (2.64)	.402 (2.74)

* Consensus score.
** Mean response.

in North Carolina is not as monotonic as in either Massachusetts or Utah. In general, then, it appears that there is less advantage to lobbyists in Oregon and Utah in developing an image of professionalism than in presenting the appearance of a well-meaning amateur whose intentions are honorable. To appear too "slick" contributes to a hostile reaction.

Interaction and Perceptual Congruence

If the data presented so far in this chapter seem to suggest that the lobbyist has the advantage in the legislator-lobbyist exchange, they should not be allowed to obscure at least one other important factor operating against the lobbyist. Lobbying, as we pointed out earlier, is a marginal occupation, whereas legislating is at least less marginal. Lobbyists do not derive much satisfaction from what they believe to be their public image. Legislators are supposed to pass laws. But what, in the mind of the public, is a lobbyist supposed to do? There is, at very least, considerable ambiguity in the pattern of behavior expected of a person filling the role of a lobbyist, and this ambiguity is a source of frustration and anxiety for lobbyists. Consequently, they, of necessity, look to legislative approval as a source of psychic satisfaction. Therefore, the perception that legislators have of lobbyists as being professional is somewhat counterbalanced by the dependence of lobbyists upon legislators for approval of their social role.

The preceding comments are based upon depth interviews with a smaller sample of lobbyists in each of the states under examination. However, our larger survey contained a question which helps to place these comments in perspective. Legislators and lobbyists were asked to estimate the feelings of various segments of the population toward lobbyists by means of a ''feeling thermometer'' calibrated in degrees from 0 to 99. The respondents were instructed to place a mark on the thermometer which roughly approximated their perception of the favorableness of others' general feeling toward lobbyists. A neutral response would thus be in the neighborhood of 50. Average responses for each group and category are given in Table 5.6.

Notice that in every state, no matter what the strength of the interest-group system, lobbyists believe that the general public has an unfavorable image of them. On the other hand, lobbyists believe that state legislators have a considerably higher opinion of them, although just how high that opinion is believed to be varies considerably from state to state. Legislators agree both that the general public has a relatively low opinion of lobbyists and that legislators have a much higher opinion of them. As we would expect, legislators in strong-lobby states indicate a more favorable attitude toward lobbyists than legislators in weak-lobby states, whose attitude toward lobbyists tends to be neutral. However, as is evident in the third column of Table 5.6, in no state do the legislators indicate that their opinion of lobbyists is as high as lobbyists seem to think it is. Significantly, the disparity between the opinions of legislators and

TABLE 5.6

Attitudes Toward Lobbyists, as Estimated by Legislators and Lobbyists

	Estimates of General Public's Attitude	Legislator's Estimate of Attitude of Other Legislators	Legislator's Own Attitude	Estimate of Lobbyists' Perception of Legislator's Own Attitude
MASSACHUSETTS				
Legislator	28.0*	56.4	54.5	55.2
Lobbyist	30.8	—	58.2	—
NORTH CAROLINA				
Legislator	26.3	55.6	50.7	55.1
Lobbyist	32.9	—	67.8	—
OREGON				
Legislator	29.1	75.5	76.0	68.2
Lobbyist	32.5	—	77.3	—
UTAH				
Legislator	30.3	63.4	64.3	62.0
Lobbyist	35.3	—	64.4	—

* Degrees on a scale from 0 (negative) to 99 (positive).

the perceptions of lobbyists is greater in weak-lobby states than in strong-lobby states. The disparity is greater, in other words, in states in which interaction between lobbyists and legislators is less frequent. A statement by Homans bears on this finding: "The more frequently men interact with one another, the more nearly alike they become in the norms they hold as they do in their sentiments and activities."[7] Thus, interaction increases not only positive evaluations but also congruence of perceptions. This is confirmed in Table 5.7, which relates the rates of interaction of legislators and

[7] Homans, p. 112.

lobbyists in all four states to the discrepancy between the legislator's attitude toward the lobbyist and the lobbyist's perception of
that attitude. In every case, the discrepancy is reduced as the rate
of interaction increases.

TABLE 5.7

Rate of Interaction and Congruence of Perception

| | RATE OF INTERACTION | | |
	Low	Medium	High
Legislators' attitude toward lobbyists	45.5*	58.1	72.1
Lobbyists' estimate of legislators' attitude	61.0	69.3	75.0
Difference	15.5	11.2	2.9

* Degrees on a scale from 0 (extremely negative), through 50 (neutral), to 99
(extremely positive). Entries are averages computed from responses of legislators
and lobbyists in all four sample states.

The basic principle that emerges is that interaction produces
favorable sentiments and congruence of perception, both of which
contribute to the effectiveness of lobbying. Those who can make
accurate predictions about the reactions of others are effective communicators. It must be remembered that lobbyists face a bias that
must be overcome, a bias built into their relationship with legislators. In experimental research dealing with the credibility of the
communicator, it has been suggested that when the target for persuasion perceives the communicator as having something to gain
from pushing his point of view and having it accepted, persuasion is
less likely to occur. When there is a reduced imputation to the agent
of persuasion of an overt attempt to influence, the chances of his
achieving an attitude change are greater. The lobbyist, of course, is
assumed by all parties to have an axe to grind. Overcoming this bias
is difficult, and it appears that expertness does not necessarily
function as well as trustworthiness in reducing the effects of this
bias. Hovland, Janis, and Kelley conclude that favorable estimates
of the fairness and trustworthiness of the source play a greater role
than favorable estimates of expertness in leading to attitude change
in the direction advocated by the source.[8] This conclusion is sub-
stantiated by the case of Oregon, the state with the strongest lob-

[8] Carl I. Hovland, Irving L. Janis, and Harold H. Kelley, *Communication and
Persuasion* (New Haven: Yale University Press, 1953), pp. 35–36.

bies. In Oregon, legislators regard lobbyists as more trustworthy than do the legislators of other states. Oregon legislators also view this characteristic as highly desirable. Trust and interaction are, of course, related. Those legislators who have less trust of lobbyists interact at a substantially lower rate than those who have more trust.

Some Relations between Images and Effects

We have implied that the persuasibility of legislators and their attitudes toward lobbyists seem to be related to the number of interactions they have with lobbyists, but that the effects of these interactions vary with the expectations of both the legislators and the lobbyists in each state. State lobbyists do not, as Milbrath observed of Washington lobbyists, worry about "over-lobbying." Indeed, the more lobbyists interact with legislators, the more likely they are to persuade them to their point of view (see Table 5.8).

TABLE 5.8

Persuasibility of Legislators and Mean
Number of Interactions Per Week

Persuasibility	Mean Interactions
Low	9.6
Medium	12.7
High	16.6

This point, that interaction aids persuasion, can be amplified by returning to the concept of direct lobbying. We noted that direct lobbying is more typical of the strong-lobby states than of the weak-lobby states. If we relate professionalism and direct lobbying, the impact of expectations upon behavior becomes somewhat clearer. By combining lobbyists' self-evaluations with the evaluations of legislators, we were able to classify lobbyists as either professional or amateur. In every state except Utah, we found that professional lobbyists are more likely than amateurs to rely upon direct rather than indirect lobbying techniques (see Table 5.9).

98   CHAPTER FIVE

This is true even of Oregon, where amateurism is the norm. Only in
Utah is there a slightly greater tendency on the part of the amateur
to interact directly.

A further check on this point can be made by examining evaluations of the effectiveness of various groups. Legislators and lob-

TABLE 5.9

Professionalism and Lobbying Technique: Percentage
of Lobbyists Relying on Direct Contact

	Massachusetts (N)	North Carolina (N)	Oregon (N)	Utah (N)
Professional	55% (128)	57% (88)	75% (116)	50% (62)
Amateur	37 (54)	36 (39)	59 (66)	53 (70)

byists were asked to list the groups they considered to be the most
influential. The groups were then ranked from most influential to
least influential based on the number of times they were mentioned by both legislators and lobbyists. On the basis of these
rankings, the list of groups was divided into quartiles, the quartile
into which a group fell thus indicating its power. As Table 5.10

TABLE 5.10

Professionalism and Power: Percentage of "Professional"
Lobbyists Regarded as "Powerful" or "Powerless"

	Powerful*	Powerless**	Difference***
Massachusetts	75%	59%	16
North Carolina	75	55	20
Oregon	60	55	5
Utah	38	39	−1

* First two quartiles.
** Last two quartiles.
*** Differences in number of percentage points.

indicates, in Massachusetts and North Carolina perceptions of
professionalism and perceptions of power are closely related; in
Oregon and Utah, however, they are not related. The presentation
of the self-image, then, is related to the ability of the lobbyist to
achieve a desired result. The wrong image (a professional image in
Oregon) can reduce the probability of success.

The Development of Institutionalized Interaction

Earlier in this chapter, we concluded that lobbyists are more effective when legislators have not developed professional norms. We pointed out that professionalism among legislators encourages the formation of ingroups which tend to exclude outsiders such as lobbyists. Now we wish to know if the obverse also holds true. Do states in which legislators do not have a high sense of professionalism exhibit a more institutionalized network of legislator-lobbyist relations?

In the strong-lobby, high-interaction, nonprofessional states, lobbyists have established a "standard operating procedure"—a set of rules of the game—to a greater extent than is true in the weak-lobby states. To an extent related to the strength of lobbies in their states, legislators are aware of these rules. Fifty percent of the Oregon legislators and 31 percent of the Utah legislators are aware of such rules, as opposed to 21 percent of the Massachusetts legislators and 23 percent of the North Carolina legislators (see Table 5.11). Thus, in Oregon and Utah, there is greater recognition among

TABLE 5.11

Perception of "Rules of the Game" by Legislators: Percentage Aware of Rules, by State and Frequency of Interaction

Rate of Interaction	Massachusetts (N)	North Carolina (N)	Oregon (N)	Utah (N)
Low	11% (121)	16% (71)	—%* (4)	25% (8)
Medium	28 (55)	29 (58)	41 (32)	22 (27)
High	40 (38)	29 (35)	54 (48)	36 (55)
All	21% (244)	23% (164)	50% (84)	31% (90)

* N too small to compute percentage.

both legislators and lobbyists of a more regularized way of doing things. The table also might seem to suggest that the development of regularized relationships increases with frequency of interaction. There are, however, obvious impediments in the way of this generalization. The perception of rules of the game is higher in Oregon, for example, than in Utah, where the rate of interaction is as high as in

Oregon. Furthermore, although few Massachusetts legislators interact frequently (16 percent), those who do interact frequently are
exceeded only by Oregon in their awareness of rules of the game.
Thus, not all of the variance in perception of rules of the game can
be explained by frequency of interaction. The general environment
of the state legislature also has an impact.

If we examine the rules of the game as described by legislators,
the contrast between weak-lobby states and strong-lobby states does
not hold up, however. In Oregon, the basic rule is to keep promises
and to be honest (see Table 5.12). In Utah, however, the basic rule is

TABLE 5.12

Descriptions of Rules by Legislators*

	Massa-chusetts	North Carolina	Oregon	Utah
Don't socialize or accept favors or invitations; keep your distance.	36%	52%	34%	47%
Be honest; keep promises.	44	19	41	6
Hear lobbyist out, but listen only to facts.	19	19	6	18
Maintain independence; don't make promises; don't reveal.	28	23	25	36
Don't imply you will take a bribe.	—**	6	12	6
(N)	(43)	(31)	(32)	(34)

* Total percentages exceed 100 due to multiple responses.
** Less than 1 percent.

to avoid social intercourse with lobbyists, to refuse social invitations
from them, and to reject personal favors from them. This is also the
basic rule in North Carolina. But, in Massachusetts, as in Oregon,
the basic rule is commitment to one's promises and honesty in one's
relationships. It appears that the legislators' rules of the game in
Utah are predicated upon the assumption of hostility between legislators and lobbyists and a suspicion on the part of legislators with
regard to the motives of lobbyists. Even though both states have
strong lobby systems, it is apparent that Utah legislators do not
view the rules of the game in a manner at all similar to that of the
Oregon legislators.

While it is true that the persuasibility of legislators is related to
the extent of their awareness of rules of the game, the highly

persuasible Utah legislators are not aware of rules to any greater degree than the legislators in the weak-lobby states (see Table 5.13). Utah is also the only state in which there is a substantial decline in perception of rules on the part of the most highly persuasible legislators. Explanations for the unusual perceptions of Utah legislators are undertaken elsewhere and need not concern us here.[9] For

TABLE 5.13

Persuasibility of Legislators and Their Perception of the Existence of Rules of the Game: Percentage Aware of Rules

Persuasibility	Massachusetts (N)	North Carolina (N)	Oregon (N)	Utah (N)
Low	29% (61)	14% (70)	33% (6)	8% (13)
Medium	24 (115)	30 (70)	50 (40)	39 (49)
High	29 (68)	29 (24)	53 (38)	29 (28)

the moment it is sufficient to observe that the institutionalization of interaction does not operate to the advantage of lobbyists in Utah as it does in the other strong-lobby state, Oregon. If we recall that Oregon legislators are most likely to consider lobbyists as honest, the importance of the institutionalization of interactions becomes apparent. Oregon legislators consider lobbyists as honest and regard honesty as the fundamental rule of the game. In Massachusetts, on the other hand, there is less of a tendency to consider lobbyists as honest, but honesty is nevertheless the basic rule. The inference is that Massachusetts legislators do not see lobbyists as conforming to the rule as much as do the Oregon legislators.

Obviously there is no full institutionalization of interactions in any of the states considered here. However, the strong-lobby states do seem to exhibit a greater degree of institutionalization than do the weak-lobby states. In Oregon, where expectations and conformity to expectations seem more clearly established, the high regard of legislators toward lobbyists and the accurate perceptions by lobbyists of this high regard contribute to a counterbalancing of the unfavorable public images which lobbyists attach to their marginal position. In states such as Massachusetts, where there is no institutionalized alternative to the negative perception of the public's feeling toward them, lobbyists are substantially more discouraged

[9] See Chapter 2.

about their work and are generally more cynical about the political process than are lobbyists in states such as Oregon. When asked how much they thought their efforts accomplished, approximately 75 percent of lobbyists in Oregon, Utah, and North Carolina reported a belief that their efforts had induced legislators at least to question a previously held position. In Massachusetts, however, only 41 percent of the lobbyists attributed to their efforts even this "minimum persuasive effect."

Services Provided by Lobbyists

Whatever their image of lobbyists, legislators are more likely to look on them as service agents than as opinion manipulators. We can dichotomize services performed by lobbyists into those involving a display of power or influence and those involving the provision of information. Typically, legislators utilize lobbyists as sources of influence in three ways: by calling upon lobbyists to influence other legislators, by calling upon lobbyists to help amass public opinion in favor of the legislator's position, and by including lobbyists in planning strategy in an effort to negotiate a bill through the legislature. The extent to which lobbyists are called upon to perform these services is indicated in Table 5.14.

This table says nothing new about the relative importance of lobbying as a whole in the various states. Oregon still ranks as the most lobbying-oriented state; Utah runs a close second; North Carolina and Massachusetts bring up the rear. However, the table does reveal some variations in the kinds of influence services likely to be performed by the lobbyists in a given state. For instance, participation by lobbyists in the planning strategy preceding the introduction of a bill is apparently a more common occurrence in Oregon and North Carolina than in Utah and Massachusetts. The lobbyist is not called upon to help to amass public opinion in Oregon as often as we might be led to believe by the relatively high frequency with which he is called upon to perform other informational services. It appears that most of the services performed by Oregon lobbyists are kept within the internal politics of the legislature. This is not true to the same extent in any other state. Indeed, the amassing of public opinion is the single item on which both sets of judges in Utah rank their state higher than Oregon.

Within the other general category of lobbyist services, the provision of information, there are two typical subcategories: the communication to the legislator of the opinions of other legislators or lobbyists and the actual conducting of research for the use of the legislator in the presentation of arguments for or against legislation. The first kind of service is, essentially, the utilization of

TABLE 5.14

Percentage of Legislators and Lobbyists
Interacting for "Influence" Services*

	Influencing Other Legislators	Mobiliz- ing Public Support	Participat- ing in Planning Strategy	(N)
MASSACHUSETTS				
Legislators	11%	17	17	(244)
Lobbyists	22%	38	36	(185)
NORTH CAROLINA				
Legislators	25%	27	39	(164)
Lobbyists	51%	65	73	(132)
OREGON				
Legislators	53%	32	65	(84)
Lobbyists	55%	46	64	(193)
UTAH				
Legislators	46%	45	42	(70)
Lobbyists	68%	65	73	(134)

* Percentages of respondents who "frequently" or "occasionally" request (or are requested to perform) a service.

lobbyists for the "nose-counting" which usually precedes any decision by the legislator concerning strategy. The second kind of service, the gathering of information through technical research, is one on which state legislators rely heavily (see Table 5.15), since, unlike members of Congress, state legislators usually do not have staff assistants to perform such research.

There is greater agreement between legislators and lobbyists that informational services are typical of the legislator-lobbyist relationship than there is that influence services are typical of the relationship. While there is a mean difference of about 21 percent between the perceptions of legislators and the perceptions of lobbyists with regard to influence services, there is a difference of only 7 percent

TABLE 5.15

Percentage of Legislators and Lobbyists
Interacting for "Informational" Services*

	Communi- cating with Other Lobbyists	Researching a Bill	(N)
MASSACHUSETTS			
Legislators	25%	46	(244)
Lobbyists	22%	43	(185)
NORTH CAROLINA			
Legislators	19%	47	(164)
Lobbyists	51%	71	(132)
OREGON			
Legislators	40%	89	(84)
Lobbyists	53%	73	(193)
UTAH			
Legislators	49%	78	(90)
Lobbyists	63%	63	(134)

*Percentages of respondents who "frequently" or "occasionally" request (or are requested to) perform a service.

between the perceptions of the two groups with respect to informational services (see Table 5.16). Only in North Carolina does the difference between the perceptions of the two groups with respect to informational services approach the magnitude of the difference

TABLE 5.16

Differences in Legislators' and Lobbyists'
Perceptions of Services Performed by Lobbyists*

	Influence	Information
Massachusetts	−17	+ 3
North Carolina	−37	−28
Oregon	− 5	+ 2
Utah	−25	+ 1

* The average differences in the number of percentage points between the answers of legislators and lobbyists reported in Tables 5.14 and 5.15. Negative signs indicate that more lobbyists than legislators believe the service is performed.

regarding influence services. Thus, when evaluating influence services, lobbyists apparently exaggerate (or legislators minimize).[10] It appears, in other words, that legislators look upon lobbyists as providers of information, but lobbyists like to think of themselves as agents of influence.

The findings reported in Tables 5.14 and 5.15 support our conclusion in Chapter 4 that lobbyists spend more of their time in administrative work than in contact work. Pedestrian as it may seem to lobbyists, it is clear that even in weak-lobby states, such as Massachusetts, they are called upon most frequently to provide legislators with facts. In strong-lobby states there is a greater amount of influence-trading, but even in these states research is the basic task. For lobbyists, the prominence of research services in their relationship with legislators means that persuasion has to be accomplished by indirect means. We noted earlier that experienced lobbyists are inclined to define their role as that of informant. Concurrently, legislators indicate a substantial preference for the services of experienced lobbyists, especially if those lobbyists have had previous governmental experience. In all states, these kinds of lobbyists are sought out for services far more often than are the inexperienced lobbyists. The experienced lobbyists frequently engage in explicit attempts to portray themselves as informants. Consider, for example, the following statement:

> Last session there were eleven people on the House Financial Affairs Committee. Five of them were freshmen. My first job was to introduce myself to them and let them know that I would be around, be at the Committee meetings, and that I am the fount of all information with respect to the insurance industry, and if they have questions they should call on me. Certainly I try to persuade them. But I try to persuade them with information.

This lobbyist is seeking to establish a relationship with legislators based solely upon his role as informant. If successful, he will have built a substantial influence base, a base founded upon the willingness of legislators to seek him out.

---

[10] When evaluating informational services, both legislators and lobbyists see lobbyists' performance in a similar manner. In Oregon and Utah, for example, more legislators than lobbyists indicate that lobbyists are called upon for research. However, the differences in perception in Oregon are relatively small, no matter whether influence or informational services are being evaluated. This would indicate a higher congruence in legislator-lobbyist perception in Oregon than in the other states. Nevertheless, it does appear that these answers are somewhat indicative of an idealization of roles.

6 THE STYLES OF LOBBYISTS

In this chapter we direct our attention to the manner in which lobbyists seek to influence the behavior of legislators and the extent to which they are able to do so. We focus on the lobbyist's and the legislator's differing perceptions of the nature and intent of the communication between them. Our initial concern is with a somewhat idealized categorization of the essential component of the message: Is it primarily informational or persuasive? A sharper distinction can be drawn with regard to the notion of "pressure." Lobbyists are supposed, according to the stereotype, to apply pressure to legislators, who, against their better judgment, give in. How accurate is this picture of the lobbying process?

Persuasion or Information

It is occasionally assumed that the lobbyist seeks primarily to reinforce rather than to change attitudes. The consequences of this assumption are (1) that most interaction occurs between two partisans—"Its [the interest group's] role became that of an auxiliary service bureau for a senator with whom it was in complete agreement"[1] —and (2) that successful lobbyists are those upon whom legislators know they can rely for accurate information, preferably information which is available most conveniently

[1] Raymond A. Bauer, Ithiel de Sola Pool, and Lewis Dexter, *American Business and Public Policy* (New York: Atherton Press, 1963), p. 357.

106

(or exclusively) from lobbyists. One lobbyist phrased the job of the informant in these words: "I try to establish a reputation for having certain . . . technical information which is otherwise unavailable to them [legislators]."

These generalizations, however, are derived from the national legislative process and may not apply to the states. In the states it may be true (1) that lobbyists communicate with opponents or undecided legislators, and (2) that successful lobbyists are those who are able to convert opponents into supporters and to firm up waverers. According to one such lobbyist: "We are trying to influence votes on certain measures. We spend most of our time trying to influence votes on legislative measures."

Our data suggest that both the informational and the conversion models contain part of the truth. In Table 6.1 we have categorized

TABLE 6.1

Legislators' and Lobbyists' Classifications of the Lobbyist's Role

	Persuader	Informant	Both	(N)
MASSACHUSETTS				
Legislators	30%	42	28	(244)
Lobbyists	54%	18	28	(185)
NORTH CAROLINA				
Legislators	20%	53	27	(164)
Lobbyists	45%	29	27	(132)
OREGON				
Legislators	26%	55	19	(84)
Lobbyists	48%	34	19	(193)
UTAH				
Legislators	29%	57	14	(90)
Lobbyists	38%	36	25	(134)

legislators and lobbyists according to whether they spend more of their time sending or receiving messages with a content perceived as either primarily informational or primarily persuasive.[2] Obviously, such a categorization of the nature of communication is idealized. Information is certainly an instrument of persuasion, and most

[2] The categorization is derived from the "purposive" and "non-purposive" distinction found in the literature of communications. See Bruce H. Westley and Malcolm S. MacLean, Jr., "A Conceptual Model for Communications Research," in James H. Campbell and Hal W. Helper, eds., Dimensions in Communication (Belmont, California: Wadsworth Publishing Co., 1965), pp. 61–62.

messages are probably a mixture of the two. Nevertheless, respondents were able to form an opinion of what the essential purpose of
lobbyists' messages is.

The table illustrates a concept fundamental to the examination of
the interaction process. It will be noticed that the nature of the
interaction is seen quite differently by the two participants. The
pattern is quite consistent from state to state. In every case, most
lobbyists classify themselves as persuaders but most legislators define themselves as receivers of information. These contrasting perceptions of the encounter can be expected to have an impact upon
the behavior of the actors. As we have argued, the nature of the
encounter is defined by the perceptions of the participants. It
stands to reason, then, that the more congruent are the perceptions
of the participants, the less ambiguous will be the encounter. In this
case, the effectiveness of the lobbyist should be related to the extent
of harmony between his perceptions and those of the legislator. In
other words, the clearer the mutual expectations of lobbyist and
legislator, the more effective the lobbyist.

For an idea of the extent of congruence in the expectations of the
two groups, let us examine the rate of interaction spent in either
information or persuasive communication (Table 6.2). We can see

TABLE 6.2

Interaction Rates of Legislators and Lobbyists
Whose Exchange Is Based on Persuasion or Information:
Percentage of Time Spent in Each Kind of Communication

	Persuasion	Information
MASSACHUSETTS		
Legislators	25%	33%
Lobbyists	46	22
NORTH CAROLINA		
Legislators	9	17
Lobbyists	33	22
OREGON		
Legislators	21	30
Lobbyists	37	25
UTAH		
Legislators	23	38
Lobbyists	33	32

that the greatest congruence concerning perception of persuasion occurs in Oregon, followed by Utah, North Carolina, and Massachusetts. Thus, the two states with the highest interaction have the greatest congruence. It will be argued shortly that Oregon and Utah are the states with the strongest groups, thus supporting the idea that a relationship exists between congruence and effectiveness. Further, the fact that there is greater congruence in states with high interaction indicates that stereotypic perceptions probably dictate the terms of an *initial* encounter, but that more accurate images develop as the interactions become more frequent. Hence, Massachusetts and North Carolina, the states with the lowest rate of interaction, are also the states with the least congruence and the least effective lobbyists. Notice also that in all four states there is greater congruence concerning informational communication. This may indicate a greater acceptance of the legitimacy of this type of communication and, incidentally, suggest an introductory chapter to a textbook for beginning lobbyists.

Pressure

We have talked about direct and indirect communications, about persuasive and informational communications, and about the creation of resources—such as credibility and expertise—which help lobbyists overcome situational barriers. The basic barrier against effective lobbying is the legislator's perception that any lobbyist has an axe to grind. He is not viewed as impartial. In spite of the fact that many legislators find lobbyists extremely helpful, they still feel the need for "objective" information. They expect lobbyists, however, to present information in the most favorable light from the lobbyist's point of view. Consequently, the basic goal of all lobbying strategy and tactics is the reduction of the effects of this inevitable bias against lobbyists.

In such a strategy, "pressure" plays a minor part. The attempted application of pressure by a lobbyist cannot create a relationship with a legislator that is satisfactory in terms of the reduction of bias. This is not to say that there are no lobbyists who rely on pressure tactics. In general, however, pressure is a word not clearly defined or understood either by legislators or lobbyists. It is difficult to nudge a conversation with a lobbyist around to the subject of pressure; and, when this is done, the interview usually deteriorates to the level of stereotypic responses. However, lobbyists do understand quite well the necessity of establishing credibility, as illustrated by the following conversation with a lobbyist:

> *Interviewer:* If someone came up to you and asked you about the pros and cons of a particular bill, would you be willing to tell the legislator the bad aspects of the bill?
>
> *Lobbyist:* Sure.
>
> *Interviewer:* Even though you supported the bill?
>
> *Lobbyist:* Yes. I am not going to try to fool you. I'm not going to be as persuasive with the other arguments as I am going to be with my own, but I will tell them to the limit of my ability the other side.

The lobbyist making these remarks is one who is frequently called upon by legislators to provide information.

After a legislator had mentioned this lobbyist as being helpful, he was asked why this was the case. He replied:

> I relied on him because I think he knows what he is talking about. I think he has expertise in his field. This is what I want from a lobbyist—information. I don't want any entertainment from them, I don't want happy talk, and so on.

Of course, the legislator may be overstating the case. As it turns out, he is frequently entertained by lobbyists. But even if this is so, the legislator rarely, if ever, associates entertainment with pressure tactics.

A typical contact with lobbyists is described in the following manner:

> Last Monday I went down to a Fiscal Committee meeting in the afternoon and that evening I heard that there was to be a gathering of legislators out at a favorite watering hole which is quite close to a motel owned by a state senator. As soon as I walked into the road house and nobody was there, I knew that they must be over at the motel. So I went to the motel, where there are usually two large units rented out to lobbyists. And sure enough, there were about eight legislators and two lobbyists sitting around drinking and telling stories and just having a convivial evening. Now this is a typical contact between legislators and lobbyists. One of the lobbyists, who is a personal friend of mine and has contributed to my campaigns, wanted to talk to me just briefly about what direction we were going to take

at our next hearing. That is all he wanted to know—what subjects we were going to cover at our next hearing. He had sat in
on the hearing that afternoon. I had not been specifically invited
to his apartment. I had just dropped in.

This account certainly does not lend support to the belief that
lobbyists "pressure" legislators. An important point is, of course,
that the lobbyist had no trouble in beginning a conversation and
eliciting information from the legislator because he was his personal
friend and had contributed to his campaign fund. The significance
of financial contributions will be discussed shortly. First, let us
consider the extent to which the exchange described above is not
typical. That is to say, let us try to ascertain how much pressure
there is in the lobbying process, and what is meant by the word.

Table 6.3 gives the percentages of legislators and lobbyists who

TABLE 6.3

Perceptions of "Pressure": Percentage of Legislators and Lobbyists
Who Believe Lobbyists Apply Pressure "All or Most" of the Time

	Legislators (N)		Lobbyists (N)	
Massachusetts	17%	(244)	34%	(185)
North Carolina	13	(164)	18	(132)
Oregon	13	(84)	14	(193)
Utah	22	(90)	28	(134)

believe that lobbyists engage in "pressure tactics" all or most of the
time. The state-by-state variations indicate that Massachusetts and
Utah are characterized by more pressure than are North Carolina
and Oregon. We might have expected perceptions of pressure by
legislators to be greatest in weak-lobby states. We would have
expected this because perceptions of pressure are related to the
hostility that legislators feel toward lobbyists, and we would expect
hostility to be greater in the weak-lobby states. However, while the
responses from Oregon and Massachusetts conform to these expectations, the responses from North Carolina and Utah do not. In
general, then, perception of pressure does not seem to be a function
of the strength of the interest-group system.

In all states, whatever the relative strengths of their interest-
group systems, a minority of both legislators and lobbyists are

aware of much pressure. In every state, however, more lobbyists than legislators describe pressure as a regular part of the legislative way of life. Perhaps some of the frustrations of being a lobbyist are expressed in this response. Notice that the Massachusetts lobbyists are unusually high in their perception of pressure. Their orientation toward pressure is typical of the cynicism they express toward the legislative process in general. In Massachusetts, 25 percent of the lobbyists, compared to a tiny smattering of lobbyists in the other states, believe that legislators listen most to "whoever brings the most pressure." Yet Massachusetts legislators, like legislators in the other states, do not share this perspective.

In Utah, a higher proportion of legislators perceive pressure than in any other state. This perception is, perhaps, part of the general distrust of lobbyists which characterizes Utah legislators. Utah legislators frequently complain about "hot-boxing" tactics on the part of lobbyists. Forty-four percent of the Utah legislators object to lobbyists "cornering" them, compared to about one fourth of the legislators in other states. The fact of the matter is that the problem of built-in biases is especially acute in Utah, and even the most well-intentioned approach by a lobbyist is likely to generate a hostile response.

Hostility and Perceptions of Pressure

Pressure is more likely to be a function of the attitude of the legislator toward a given lobbyist than a function of any overt behavior on the part of the lobbyist. When asked what organizations most often exert pressure, both legislators and lobbyists mentioned education and labor organizations far more than any others. In practically all cases, the respondent "had heard" of education and labor exerting pressure but had no direct evidence of such pressure. In most cases the kind of pressure which these organizations were said to have exerted was electoral. Threats to defeat legislators at the polls were thought to be very common in the repertoires of education and labor lobbyists. When asked if these lobbyists were active in trying to defeat legislators, another lobbyist responded:

> I think the labor lobbyists are. I think they do it openly. Of
> course, they refine it down more than the "reward our friends and

punish our enemies" sort of thing. But they are the most out-spoken about it. The teachers' associations make noises like they would like to do more than that, but most of us don't.

To the same question, a legislator replies:

I have seen some signs of some groups like teachers that say, "All right, if that's the way you feel, we'll remember it the next time."

Since perceptions of pressure are almost always related to ele-ments of the electoral process, it is not surprising that labor and education lobbyists are the groups most frequently assumed to exert pressure. Both organizations contain more members than most of the other interest groups in the states; and, in all states except North Carolina (where labor is virtually impotent), both organizations are highly active and highly vocal. However, it is important to point out that most of the comments attributing pressure tactics to labor and education lobbyists are based on nothing more than hearsay evidence. In reality, labor and education lobbyists know little more about pressure tactics than any other lobbyists; everybody assumes, however, that these lobbyists must be making threats. Perception of pressure, as we mentioned earlier, is a function of legislative sympa-thy. If the legislator believes that labor lobbyists, because they have the electoral manpower, are oriented toward the application of pressure, then even the most innocent comment by the lobbyist might be misperceived. If we assume that Democrats are more sympathetic with organized labor than are Republicans, we can get a clearer idea of the perceptual basis of pressure. Since labor lobbyists and Democratic legislators cooperate more closely than do labor lobbyists and Republican legislators, we would expect Repub-lican legislators to have more hostility toward labor lobbyists and to perceive greater pressure emanating from those lobbyists than Demo-cratic legislators. Table 6.4 reveals that this is indeed the case. In every state except North Carolina, where labor is not very active, the Republicans perceive the most pressure.[3] Perceptions of pres-sure, therefore, do not appear to be necessarily based upon any empirical evidence on the part of legislators. Rather, they appear to

[3] By the same token, as our research also revealed, Democratic legislators are more likely than Republican legislators to attribute pressure to business lob-byists.

be more firmly rooted in the attitude of the legislator toward the lobbyist.[4]

There is a certain mythology of pressure which grows up around active organizations with large memberships. Contrary to this mythology, the electoral activities of organized labor are somewhat

TABLE 6.4

Legislators' Perception of Labor Lobbyists' Use of Pressure
Tactics: Percentages by State and Party Affiliation

	Republicans	(N)	Democrats	(N)	Total for State	(N)
Massachusetts	67%	(75)	43%	(169)	51%	(244)
North Carolina	13	(15)	15	(149)	15	(164)
Oregon	75	(40)	52	(44)	63	(84)
Utah	67	(38)	39	(52)	42	(90)
All States	60	(168)	34	(409)		

circumscribed, even in industrialized Massachusetts. Of course, interest groups, especially organized labor, contribute to campaigns; but this activity is unlikely to be intended or interpreted as a threat not to contribute if the legislator fails to cooperate with the interest group.

The Creation and Use of Obligations

If the basic goal in lobbying strategy is to create good will, fear-arousing communications would be a poor choice of weapons. On the other hand, any activity which does create good will is useful, and certainly the contribution of money to a candidate's campaign should be viewed in this light. The extent of campaign support on the part of lobbyists varies substantially. In the weak-lobby states, less than a majority of legislators have received financial help in their campaigns from interest groups (32 percent of legislators in Massachusetts and 42 percent of legislators in North Carolina). In Oregon, however, 58 percent of legislators have received help; in Utah, 62 percent have received financial support.

[4] On this point, see Frank Bonilla, ''When Is Petition 'Pressure?' '' *Public Opinion Quarterly*, 20 (Spring 1956), 46–48.

The wisdom of this strategy is not entirely obvious. It is true that those legislators who have received support during their candidacy are more likely to interact with lobbyists than those who do not. As Table 6.5 indicates, however, the differences in rates of interaction

TABLE 6.5

Relationship between the Receipt of Campaign Contributions from Interest Groups and Legislators' Interaction, in Percentages

| | INTERACTION | | | |
	Low	Medium	High	(N)
MASSACHUSETTS				
Received support	42%	32	26	(82)
Received no support	51%	38	11	(162)
NORTH CAROLINA				
Received support	33%	40	27	(69)
Received no support	48%	33	18	(95)
OREGON				
Received support	6%	35	59	(49)
Received no support	3%	43	54	(35)
UTAH				
Received support	7.%	29	64	(57)
Received no support	12%	30	58	(33)

are greatest in the weak-lobby states. In strong-lobby states, while the legislators who have received support do interact at a somewhat higher rate, the differences are not very great. Still, since rate of interaction is closely associated with persuasibility and a generally favorable attitude toward lobbyists, any device which increases interaction is of considerable value to lobbyists.

The important point here is that support in the electoral arena can be used by the lobbyist to create feelings of obligation on the part of the legislator—at least the obligation to give the lobbyist an audience. Electoral support is not given with the implied threat of withdrawal, but, if the support has been continuous, it can be drawn upon by the lobbyist as a source of obligation. One lobbyist, whose organization contributes heavily to legislators' campaigns, talks about the utilization of this obligation:

If it is an important bill, one that we just about have to get passed, usually I'll go to somebody and say, "Look, this is one I have to have and I want you to vote on this bill." I am calling in a debt. However, I don't use this very often because you can only use it once in a while. And you can only use it on a legislator once during a session. It is best to avoid an overt feeling of obligation, but every lobbyist does have certain legislators that he can go to if he really needs a vote. I'll probably do this two or three times during a normal session. You just don't put on the pressure every day. You save it until you need it.

I will also ask a legislator to get a vote that I can't get. This is the kind of pressure that you use, but you just don't go to a legislator and say 'You do it or else.' That is the poorest tactic you can use. Remember that we know most of these people very well, and in some cases have gotten them to run for office. We have worked with them in their campaigns. Even so, if I go to him and he says "I can't do it," then I'll say, "Okay, I'll get somebody else," and forget it. You don't do it by using threats or being cute. You do not campaign against them. If they are consistently against you, they know that we would like to see them defeated, and they know that we will try to get somebody to run against them, but that is as far as it goes. I would never say to a legislator that I will try to find a candidate to oppose him, but the feeling is there.

The lobbyist recalled that during the debate on a critical bill, there was one legislator who was opposed to the point of view of the interest group and could have killed the bill if he made a speech against it. The lobbyist continued:

I knew he was against it, but I had just enough votes provided he didn't say anything. I went to him and said, "I want a personal favor from you. I don't want you to speak against this bill." He didn't, and the bill passed by two votes. This was the personal favor he gave me, just not to say anything. He voted against the bill, but he didn't take three or four more votes with him, which he would have done if he had spoken.

This is the kind of behavior which lobbyists speak of when they think of pressure. In this case, the legislator did not actually perceive the request as pressure because he was approached by a friendly lobbyist who made a request of him on a personal basis. Therefore, the legislator did not object to having his debt called in. Notice that the lobbyist treats obligations created by campaign work almost as if they were currency. Once the obligation is utilized, it cannot be ''spent'' again.

Response to Pressure

What happens if the legislator does not respond favorably to the lobbyist's request for a commitment and the lobbyist continues to press for that commitment? The result is likely to be unfortunate. As an example, consider the case of the Utah Education Association. In Utah, legislators believe that education lobbyists apply pressure more frequently than labor lobbyists. This is the only state in which this is true (except, of course, for North Carolina). In addition, 61 percent of the lobbyists in Utah (compared to 7 percent in Massachusetts, 21 percent in North Carolina, and 55 percent in Oregon) also identify education as a pressure-oriented interest group. There is also more interest in educational matters among all lobbyists in Utah than in other states. Whether or not they represent education associations, lobbyists in Utah often talk to legislators about educational issues. About half of all the Utah lobbyists talk about education frequently, compared to one third of the lobbyists in other states. Further, there are more education lobbyists on the job in Utah than in any other state. It is clear, therefore, that education is a particularly salient issue in Utah.

This does not necessarily mean, however, that education lobbyists are the Utah legislator's primary source of information about education. In order to put the activity of education lobbyists in perspective, let us examine Table 6.6, which records the responses of legislators asked to list the people with whom they have discussed

TABLE 6.6

Legislators' Sources of Information about Education*

	Massachusetts (N = 244)	North Carolina (N = 164)	Oregon (N = 84)	Utah (N = 90)
Colleagues	82%	87%	81%	84%
Education lobbyists	33	43	58	44
Business leaders	30	53	38	39
Government officials	31	53	45	37
Party leaders	32	31	19	38

* Total percentages exceed 100 because of multiple responses.

educational problems. In all states, legislators are likely to discuss education most frequently with their legislative colleagues. Still, in the strong-lobby states, Oregon and Utah, education lobbyists rank a clear second to other legislators; however, in the weak-lobby states, Massachusetts and North Carolina, they do not rank as highly. In North Carolina, for example, education lobbyists rank behind business leaders and government officials. In Massachusetts, education lobbyists rank about the same as do other sources of information. Notice the particularly strong position of education lobbyists in Oregon in comparison to party leaders. Political parties in Oregon are undisciplined and exert little influence on the votes of legislators. Here we have an especially good illustration of the strength of interest groups in the absence of strong parties.

The appearance of the interest group in Utah as the second most prominent source of information about education might lead us to expect the education lobbyist in Utah to be quite effective. But we should recall that the method of presentation of the Utah education lobbyists is viewed by legislators as aggressive, as characterized by pressure tactics. In Table 6.7, we can see that there is a relationship

TABLE 6.7

Relation between Legislators' Belief that They Were "Pressured" by Education Lobbyists and Their Attitude toward Education Goals: Percentage Favoring Increased Education Budget

	Massachusetts (N)	North Carolina (N)	Oregon (N)	Utah (N)
Felt pressure	66% (17)	3% (34)	15% (46)	6% (54)
Felt no pressure	90 (227)	17 (130)	37 (38)	14 (36)

between the perception of pressure and the attitude of the legislator toward the goals of the organization perceived as exerting the pressure. In every state, those legislators who believe they have been pressured by education lobbyists are less likely than those who have felt no pressure to support the financial goals of the education association. One should be careful, however, in interpreting these findings in terms of cause and effect. It certainly cannot be argued that those legislators who feel pressured are disinclined to support educational goals *because* of this pressure. It is equally plausible to argue that, because they are hostile toward education's goals, they feel themselves pressured when approached by education lobbyists.

In Utah, for example, where Republicans feel more pressure from education than Democrats (74 percent of Republicans gave this response, compared to 51 percent of Democrats), Republicans are also less inclined than Democrats to support higher education budgets.[5] Yet, when we control for party in Utah, we find that the relationship between perception of pressure and hostility toward education remains unchanged.[6] No matter what party legislators belong to, those who believe pressure is being brought to bear against them are more likely than others to react with hostility toward the perceived source of pressure.

Even among Utah legislators who do not perceive education interest groups as applying pressure, however, there is less support for an increase in education budgets than among nonpressured legislators in any other state. It can also be shown that in terms of outputs support of education in Utah is low in comparison to other states. For example, in 1966, Utah expended $351 per pupil, compared to $518 in Oregon, $465 in Massachusetts, and $296 in North Carolina. On eight measures of output applying to education, Utah ranks last, or next to last, on five.[7] Indeed, Salisbury includes Utah among those states which "single out education for particularly penurious treatment."[8] It might well be argued that the general environmental and cultural structure of Utah determines the product of its legislature and that the activity of the Utah Education Association makes no difference whatsoever.[9] This would mean that, no matter what the lobbyists do, the output of the legislature is

[5] In the other states, there is no clear Democratic-Republican split among legislators on the perception of the amount of pressure exerted by education lobbyists. Both parties in the other states see about the same amount of pressure. Thus, although Massachusetts is a pressure-oriented state, education is not perceived as especially pressure oriented.

[6] Among Republicans, 14 percent of those feeling pressure from the Utah Education Association supported an increased education budget, compared to 30 percent of those who felt no pressure. For Democrats, the percentages were 28 and 42, respectively.

[7] The measures are public school expenditures per pupil, public school expenditures per capita, public school expenditures per $1,000 of personal income, number of students per teacher, average teachers' salaries, number of students per room, percent increase in teachers' salaries (1953–1963), percent increase in public school expenditures (1953–1963).

[8] Robert H. Salisbury, "State Politics and Education," in Herbert Jacob and Kenneth N. Vines, eds., *Politics in the American States* (Boston: Little, Brown and Co., 1965), p. 356.

[9] See, for example, Thomas R. Dye, *Politics, Economics, and the Public* (Chicago: Rand McNally & Co., 1966).

pretty well established. The techniques of lobbying would therefore be of minimum consequence. At any rate, we can speculate that the activity of the Utah education lobbyist at least does not improve a generally discouraging situation. Whether or not a perception of pressure is a product of a legislator's already hostile attitude, it is certainly true that an organization which becomes known as a "pressure group" is likely to have little positive effect upon legislative decision making. In lobbying, as in all human communications, the best technique of interaction is to minimize hostility.

Why Lobbyists Cannot Threaten Legislators

In order for a fear-arousing communication to be effective in producing an attitude change, or at least a change in overt behavior, the communication must create an emotional tension sufficiently intense to constitute a state of drive; at the same time, the communication must offer some evidence that the acceptance of the premise of the communication will lead to a reduction of this tension. Another important requirement is that the reduction of tension should follow immediately from the arousal of tension. These conditions do not obtain in the legislator-lobbyist encounter. If a lobbyist tells a legislator that he will utilize the resources of his group to defeat the legislator at the next election, what evidence can be presented that the threat can actually be carried out? The legislator knows that it is beyond the abilities of any organized group to guarantee with any degree of certainty that its members will automatically respond to the suggestions of the leaders. Further, a lot of time may elapse between the threat and the actual execution of the threat, making it possible for the legislator to engage in fence-mending if he feels it is necessary.

The electoral threat is the only type of fear-arousing communication that legislators and lobbyists perceive as available to the lobbyists. Other kinds of threats, such as defeating legislation that the legislator is concerned about or keeping the legislator off committees upon which he wishes to serve, are not perceived by either legislators or lobbyists as being possibilities. The only threat available, therefore, is one that is not immediate to the situation and, in any case, is not clearly demonstrable as being realistic. Of course, the extent to which legislators actually believe that lobbyists can exert influence in the electoral process varies with the personal characteristics of the legislator, especially with his experience. Inexperienced legislators express more concern with the electoral activities of lobbyists than do more experienced ones. In assessing the potential effectiveness of the electoral threat, an experienced lobbyist realistically assumes that the chances of the threat's success are dependent upon the perception of the legislator, as opposed to the realities of the situation. Knowing that threatening to defeat a legislator is generally unwise, a lobbyist notes:

> . . . the old-timers take it in stride. Freshmen sometimes get a little sand in their shoes on it—get a little excited because they feel it is a life-and-death type of thing. Generally speaking, I think the freshmen respond to it more than the others. For example, if you publicize a person's voting record, a freshman might look at it and say, "Well, I was with him on such-and-such a bill and against him on such-and-such a bill." But the experienced legislators will generally just throw it in the wastebasket.

Throwing a brochure in a wastebasket is, of course, a less hostile reaction than throwing a lobbyist out of the office, but it is of the same nature. Fear-arousing materials not only fail to increase the effectiveness of the communication, they actually decrease the chances of its success, as we have seen.

The clearest result of threatening communications is the production of a defensive response, a response which mitigates against success by producing negative reactions toward the communicator. If the legislator feels that the lobbyist is trying to frighten him, he will probably deliberately reject the conclusion of the lobbyist as a way of expressing his aggression toward him. Thus, resistance to the communicator's recommendations is increased by a threat which the lobbyist cannot make real. In one state, lobbyists frequently recall one of their colleagues who was observed threatening a legislator with electoral defeat. The episode is looked upon as an example of stupidity, and the lobbyist—although hardly an amateur—is viewed as an "outsider." As one lobbyist explains, "Once you have closed the door, you have no further access to this individual. Once you've threatened an individual, there is no possibility of winning in the future."

Pressure and Persuasion

Both legislators and lobbyists make a distinction between pressure and persuasion. Pressure is oriented toward the infliction of punishment for undesirable behavior; persuasion is a substantially more low-keyed type of appeal. In a previous chapter, we categorized legislators and lobbyists according to their perception of the kinds of communications they received or transmitted. The respondents were typed as either persuaders, informants, or those who divided their time between the two forms of communications. Although lobbyists are not viewed as impartial sources of information, legislators are more likely than lobbyists themselves to view the communications of lobbyists as informational. The lobbyist himself is more likely to see his role as that of persuader. In spite of these differences in perception, both legislators and lobbyists believe that persuasive activities are far more prevalent than pressure activities. The exception here is the Massachusetts lobbyist, who, in accordance with his generally pressure-oriented perceptions, believes that pressure is more characteristic than persuasion of his legislative system.

We may think of pressure as the most intense and threatening form of communication, and of information as the least threatening, with persuasion resting somewhere between the two. In advancing a persuasive argument, the lobbyist is attempting to induce a behavior change by advocating the acceptance of a certain point of view rather than merely conveying information. Although it may use informational communications for its own purposes, persuasive communication goes beyond informational communication by explicitly advocating the acceptance of a particular position.

The lobbyist's persuasive technique can be either "rational" or "emotional." Rational persuasion draws heavily upon factual information and avoids appeals to sentiment. Lobbyists representing organizations such as insurance companies are likely to rely on rational persuasion. While the regulation of insurance might mean life or death for the insurance industry itself, it is not likely that insurance legislation will excite the antagonism of many opposing lobbyists or that a legislator will link a given piece of insurance legislation with a previously established ideological set. Lobbyists for labor unions or civil rights groups, on the other hand, frequently phrase their persuasive arguments in terms of emotional appeals by trying to link a given legislative situation to "good" or "bad" symbols. For example, a legislator might be generally committed to the abstract ideal of civil liberties but opposed to an explicit piece of legislation designed, in the eyes of the lobbyist, to increase the civil rights of a portion of the population. The lobbyist's persuasive technique in this case would be to try to link the particular piece of legislation to the general ideological position of the legislator. The lobbyist would do this on the assumption that the attitudes of the legislator toward the legislation would shift in the direction of the generalized belief once the relation between the two was established. Whether he uses rational or emotional persuasion, however, the lobbyist stops short of any statement implying adverse consequences for the legislator if the position of the lobbyist is not accepted.

Persuasion, Information, and Effect

The question arises whether purely informational communication is more effective or less effective in influencing the position of a legislator than purely persuasive communication. Table 6.8, which relates legislators' persuasibility with their perception of the nature or purpose of the communication they receive, indicates that in general those legislators who believe that lobbyists are trying to persuade them are less likely to be influenced than those who believe otherwise. This finding is generally supportive of various experiments that have recorded greater attitude change when there is less of an imputation to the agent of persuasion of an intent to influence.[10]

However, the purely informational communication is not necessarily the most effective persuasive technique. Looking at the responses to the least demanding persuasive result, the questioning of a previously held position, we find that only among Massachusetts legislators is the purely informational communication the most effective one. In every other state, those legislators who perceive

---

[10] See, for example, Elaine Walster and Leon Festinger, "The Effectiveness of 'Overhead' Persuasive Communications," *Journal of Abnormal and Social Psychology*, 65 (1962), 395–402; and Leon Festinger and Nathan Maccoby, "On Resistance to Persuasive Communications," *Journal of Abnormal and Social Psychology*, 68 (1964), 359–366.

communications as a combination of persuasion and information are those most likely to be persuaded to question a previously held position. Except in Utah, legislators who perceive lobbyist communication as this combination also respond more highly in the in-

TABLE 6.8

Legislators' Perception of the Purpose of Communication and Their Persuasibility: Percentage Indicating They Have "Frequently" or "Occasionally" Been Influenced

| | Extent of Influence | | |
*Perception of Communication**	Question a previously held position	Lean more toward the views of the lobbyist	Change from one position to another
MASSACHUSETTS			
Persuade (74)	30%	28	26
Equal (68)	31%	29	37
Inform (102)	39%	36	30
NORTH CAROLINA			
Persuade (33)	21%	21	12
Equal (44)	27%	23	18
Inform (87)	18%	17	20
OREGON			
Persuade (22)	32%	37	51
Equal (16)	69%	63	63
Inform (46)	43%	39	52
UTAH			
Persuade (26)	27%	38	46
Equal (13)	54%	31	46
Inform (51)	30%	30	39

* Legislators' characterizations of communications from lobbyists as purely persuasive, equally persuasive and informational, or purely informational.

termediate category of persuasive result—leaning more in the direction of the lobbyist. In Utah, legislators respond favorably to pure persuasion in both the intermediate category of result and the highest category—conversion from one point of view to another. Thus, although overt persuasion is generally a poor lobbying technique, it seems to be better suited to the Utah legislature than to any other.

It is to be expected, of course, that the type of communication which proves to be most effective will vary with the audience. For example, one-sided communications are generally more effective with less educated audiences.[11] In the case of lobbying, the success of a technique varies to some extent with the legislative arena in which the technique is used. In Massachusetts, for instance, the purely informational approach is best, but, in Utah, the persuasive approach seems to be most effective. In North Carolina and Oregon, there is a tendency for legislators to respond more favorably to a combination of types of communication. This is especially true in Oregon. Although only sixteen Oregon legislators categorized communication as being equally persuasive and informative, these legislators are substantially more persuadable than either those who perceive communication as purely persuasive or those who perceive communication as purely informational. In all cases, however, the information-oriented legislators are more persuadable than the persuasion-oriented legislators. It apears, therefore, that in Oregon the introduction of persuasive techniques is more tolerable from the point of view of the legislator than it is in the other states. Oregon legislators are willing to be the object of persuasive communication as long as it is partially informative; they are unwilling, however, to devote an entire interactive episode to listening to pleas for attitude change unaccompanied by concrete information. In Massachusetts, by contrast, legislators wish to avoid any exposure to persuasion, except when the attitude change demanded of them is most extreme.

In spite of these interstate variations, a general conclusion emerges: lobbyists ought to avoid purely persuasive arguments; the best chance of success rests with those lobbyists who are able to project an image containing elements of both informational and persuasive communication. The irony is that fewer legislators categorize lobbyist communication as a mixture of the two types than as purely one type or the other. This is especially true in Oregon. Here, though the most effective technique is clearly the combination, fewer legislators say they customarily receive this type of communication than say they receive either one of the other types.

Similar discrepancies between the effectiveness of a technique and the number of legislators describing lobbyist communications as characterized by that technique occur in the other states. Thus, in

[11] Carl Hovland, Arthur Lumsdaine, and Fred Sheffield, *Experiments on Mass Communication* (Princeton, N.J.: Princeton University Press, 1949).

Massachusetts, where informational communications are the most effective ones, the percentage of legislators perceiving lobbyist communication as informational is lower than in any other state. In Massachusetts a little less persuasion and a bit more information would improve the effectiveness of communications. In Oregon, on the other hand, a little less information and a bit more persuasion would have a similar result, according to the perceptions of legislators.

Further light may be shed upon the effectiveness of methods of approach by an examination of the perception of lobbyists (see Table 6.9). We noted earlier that, while legislators most frequently categorize lobbyist communication as informational, lobbyists are

TABLE 6.9

Lobbyists' Perception of Their Communicative Role and Their Estimates of Effects: Percentage Believing They Have "Frequently" or "Occasionally" Influenced a Legislator

| | *Extent of Influence* | | |
*Perception of Role**	Question a previously held position	Lean more toward the views of the lobbyist	Change from one position to another
MASSACHUSETTS			
Persuade (100)	56%	43	25
Equal (54)	32%	25	14
Inform (33)	62%	50	35
NORTH CAROLINA			
Persuade (59)	80%	73	35
Equal (35)	69%	63	49
Inform (38)	76%	71	35
OREGON			
Persuade (93)	86%	63	41
Equal (34)	67%	58	42
Inform (66)	75%	63	40
UTAH			
Persuade (51)	79%	69	49
Equal (34)	72%	55	43
Inform (48)	79%	71	52

* Lobbyists' characterizations of communications initiated by them as purely persuasive, equally persuasive and informational, or purely informational.

inclined to categorize their information as persuasive. Thus, in every state, most legislators believe they are receiving information but most lobbyists believe they are transmitting persuasion. Furthermore, lobbyists are inclined to put a considerably higher value than legislators upon pure persuasion. Lobbyists who define their communication with legislators in terms of persuasion tend to attribute greater attitude change to this communication than lobbyists who categorize their communication as informational attribute to that kind of communication. This evaluation, as we have seen, is not shared by legislators.

A striking contrast between the perceptions of legislators and lobbyists can be observed if we examine the beliefs of those lobbyists who define their communications as divided equally between information and persuasion. In most cases, these are lobbyists who believe they are the least efficacious, even though the evidence from legislators is that this is the most effective technique. Notice, for example, the responses of the Oregon lobbyists. In each case, those lobbyists who define their communication as a mixture attribute less success to their efforts than do the legislators who define communications as a mixture. This is true even though lobbyists generally overestimate the effectiveness of their communications. Furthermore, whereas it is clear that the mixed approach is especially successful in Oregon, fewer lobbyists in this state than any other employed this technique.

Most lobbyists believe they are persuaders, and perhaps it is natural for them to be influenced by their definition of their communicative role when estimating the effectiveness of communicative techniques. On the other hand, it is possible that lobbyists feel the anxiety of communicating in an unequal situation and thus are compelled toward persuasion. In a situation in which both communicators are equal in terms of influence and information, presumably there would be less of a need for overt attempts at persuasion. This point is especially well illustrated in the case of Massachusetts. In Massachusetts, where more lobbyists are persuaders and fewer lobbyists are informants than in any other state, those lobbyists who do see themselves as communicators of information also believe that they are more effective than lobbyists using other techniques, an evaluation shared by the legislators. Therefore, we have some evidence as to the source of the frustration of Massachusetts lobbyists we discussed earlier. Most of these lobbyists define themselves as persuaders but seem to recognize the futility of this approach. If they could be relied upon by legislators as a source of information, their effectiveness would, in all probability, increase. The difficulty is, of course, one of access. How is it possible for lobbyists to increase informational communication when, as is the case in Massachusetts, legislators rarely seek them out as a source of information? Most of the interaction between legislators and lobbyists in Massachusetts is initiated by the lobbyists with the intention of persuasion.

It is generally true that legislators who define lobbyists' communications as informational are more likely to initiate communication with lobbyists than are legislators who define lobbyists' communications as persuasive. Perhaps the problem is not so much in the actual content of the communication as in the circumstances surrounding the transmission of the communication. If the legislator approaches the lobbyist, he is doing so for the purpose of obtaining information. When the lobbyist supplies information under these circumstances, the legislator is less likely to think himself the object of persuasive efforts, even though he may well be. The basic problem in the interactions between legislators and lobbyists is that while legislators wish to be informed and are willing to accept a reasonable dosage of persuasion if it accompanies information, lobbyists appear to be trying too hard to persuade. The optimal dosage of persuasion is less than the dosage normally applied by lobbyists.

Approaches to Supporters and Opponents

Lobbyists in general spend more time talking to legislators with whom they are in fundamental agreement than they do in talking to opponents. This is true even of those lobbyists who define their role as persuader. Table 6.10 plots the role orientation of lobbyists against the kind of legislator with whom they are in contact most frequently. It can be seen immediately that no lobbyist spends most of his time talking to opposing legislators. In the weak-lobby states, in fact, most lobbyists do not even bother to talk to neutral legislators. In these states, even though the nature of the typical communication is persuasive, the typical interaction is between two partisans.

The purpose of persuasion, thus, is not necessarily to cause a complete reversal of attitude on the part of legislators. Rather, the

TABLE 6.10

Communicative Role Orientations of Lobbyists and Type of Legislator
with Whom They Most Frequently Interact

	Massachusetts	North Carolina	Oregon	Utah
PERSUADE	Supporters	Supporters	Neutrals	Neutrals-Supporters
EQUAL	Supporters	Supporters	Supporters	Neutrals
INFORM	Neutrals	Neutrals-Supporters	Neutrals	Neutrals

lobbyist's primary concern is often to convince a legislator who is generally friendly to the lobbyist's point of view to become an active participant in the legislative struggle. The overwhelming majority of lobbyists who spend most of their time talking to supporters do so because they want these supporting legislators to line up further support. They are trying to persuade them to become auxiliary lobbyists. When a persuasion-oriented lobbyist is talking to a supportive legislator, much of the conversation is related not to the merits of a bill, but to the role the legislator can play or is willing to play in contributing to the defeat or passage of the bill.

Few experienced and skilled lobbyists spend their time in the futile endeavor of trying to convert a dedicated opponent. A lobbyist who has had twenty years of experience in the field of private electric power explains:

> There is no point in me going in and trying to change an out-and-out public-power advocate. I might try to help a person make up his mind, but there is no point in trying to convert a person who already has a strong opinion. I would be wasting my time in trying to change their minds, especially in the limited time available during a legislative session. And if you've been around very long you can be pretty sure who your friends are, judging from what they have done in the past. You know who the people are who voted for your legislation. You can go down through the legislative calendar and pretty well identify individuals who will, or should, support your legislation, and you work more closely with them.

In other words, when attempting to influence an opposing legislator, a lobbyist relies on indirect methods. His object is to find someone who has access to the opponent. Of course, if the opponent is known to be firm in his convictions, the experienced lobbyist knows that no approach will be successful.

In many cases, however, lobbyists believe that opposing legislators are reacting not so much to the substance of the legislation as to the lobbyist personally. They frequently interpret opposition as a difficulty in communications rather than as a problem of ideology. Thus, a lobbyist explains:

> If I find someone I am having a difficult time getting through to with my point of view, I will try to figure out if there is any other member of the legislature who does agree with my particular point of view and see if I can persuade this legislator to find out what is bothering the fellow.

When it is necessary to rely upon indirect lobbying, the preferred
mediating agent is almost always another legislator. However, lobbyists will frequently try to buttress the work of other legislators
with contacts by influential constituents. When the lobbyist is unable to persuade a legislator to lobby for him, constituents become
the major agent of mediation. One lobbyist elaborates upon this
technique:

> I knew certain legislators who would just close the door on
> anyone representing the Oregon Education Association. Know-
> ing this, I had to contact people back in their constituency at
> home and indicate to them that I was not making any headway.
> I would try to find out if there was anyone in the legislator's area
> who might be able to contact him and sit down with him to ex-
> plain what the issues are and why he should favor my position.
> It might be a church member or an old school chum or even a
> relative. Sometimes it works and sometimes it doesn't.

Lobbyists are convinced that the degree of success in their use of
a third person to influence a potentially opposing legislator will
depend upon their ability to assess the peculiar characteristics of
the target of their efforts. Thus, they try to learn something of the
backgrounds and personal characteristics of these legislators. According to one lobbyist who is especially concerned with understanding the personal characteristics of legislators:

> I don't mean to suggest that I have any secret files or anything,
> but by the time the legislature meets I will have a thumbnail
> sketch on these guys, although it is not as formalized as it should
> be. But I will know what the guy does, his wife's name, how many
> children he has, what his interests are, if he has been president
> of the Kiwanis Club, what his hobbies are. I will go to our local
> people in his area and ask them for an appraisal of this guy.

Such information is used, of course, not only for selecting the
proper intermediary, but also in direct lobbying. For example, the
lobbyist quoted above indicated that one of the things he likes to
learn about legislators is whether or not they like to drink. If they
are teetotalers, he is careful to avoid any excessive use of alcohol in
their presence. Experienced lobbyists prefer to think of this sort of
information as useful primarily when direct communication has
been impeded.

Direct communication is more likely to flow toward neutrals than
toward supporters, especially in the strong-lobby states. In these

states there is more contact between lobbyists and legislators who have not yet made up their minds than between lobbyists and legislators who have made up their minds in the lobbyist's favor. This contact is almost invariably direct, and it is this sort of contact which the lobbyists believe to be a test of their skills in interpersonal communication. They like to talk to supporting legislators primarily when they are having communication problems. In a sense, then, the use of a third party is an admission of the lobbyist's inability to handle the situation. In contrast, many of the experienced lobbyists take great pride in their interaction with undecided legislators. First, the lobbyist makes sure that the sympathetic legislators understand the nature of the legislation. After that, as one lobbyist put it:

> Your next step is to find those people who are not committed pro or con and try to bring them over to your side. There aren't enough people who fundamentally agree with any one thing unless they are talked to and told the merits and demerits of the proposal.

The basic reason that lobbyists give for spending more of their time talking to undecided legislators is that these legislators are easiest to convince. This assumption dovetails nicely, of course, with the reason given by lobbyists for avoiding opponents. Lobbyists believe that neutral legislators have an open mind and are willing to listen. The willingness of a legislator to listen to a lobbyist is believed to be fundamental to success. Thus, the elaborate devices which lobbyists resort to in order to achieve access to opponents are unnecessary when neutral legislators are the lobbyists' target.

Whether or not a lobbyist will define a legislator as an opponent depends upon two factors. In the first place, the legislator's position must be well known. If it is not, lobbyists who are actually opponents might contact the legislator and become aware of his position only after the communication has been initiated. In the second place, the position of the legislator must be unequivocal and not subject to negotiation. In the words of one legislator:

> I've been in here, in the legislature, six years and so I have built up a record of positions in particular areas. Therefore, on a great many specific items lobbyists or interest groups have the right to expect me to follow a consistent position on a good many bills that I've supported or opposed over these six years. In many instances I am not sought out by a lobbyist for some interests

because they know that I have a well-defined point of view. These viewpoints over a period of years become self-evident to lobbyists and a good many stay away from me.

On the other hand, such a legislator is frequently approached when the issues are not so clearly defined:

> Every once in a while there are bills that concern a particular industry or a particular sector of the economy which are not as great a public concern, and here, where the average legislator is not inclined to have strong views one way or the other, is when a lobbyist may be able to get in touch with you and persuade you that you ought to be on his side.

But the perceptions of legislators and lobbyists are in accord on the futility of direct attempts by a lobbyist to influence the position of an opposing legislator whose views are both well known and firm. Only the beginning lobbyist does not share in this perception. That changing an opponent's mind is a very small part of the lobbying process is one of the most difficult lessons for the beginning lobbyist to learn.

"Public" and "Private" Legislation

The legislator quoted above is raising a point that relates to rational and emotional techniques of persuasion. It frequently happens that views on a particular piece of legislation reach such a level of intensity that positions become inflexible. This kind of legislation is usually linked to a broader ideological position that is not subject to manipulation. In these situations, legislators generally perceive the "broader public" to be involved, and, unless a given lobbyist can relate his position to the legislator's perception of the values of this broader public, his chances of influencing the legislator are not very great. Legislation which is of a technical or limited nature, however, provides a better field for the intrigues of lobbyists, because legislators do not relate such "private" legislation to a given image of the public interest. In such legislative situations, the legislator has more maneuverability and can usually be approached more readily by lobbyists. In general, the narrower the scope of a piece of legislation, the greater the opportunity for the lobbyist to intervene in the decision-making process. In Oregon, for example, most of the legislation involving insurance matters is sufficiently limited in scope to reduce substantially the possibility that the general public will become aroused. Frequently, therefore, legislation is introduced in the Oregon legislature at the request of the insurance lobbyist. Under these circumstances the chances of any strenuous opposition being aroused are not very great. By contrast, the insurance industry in Massachusetts is symbolically identified as being intimately involved in the allocation of broader resources. A conspicuous group of Massachusetts legislators—aligned with the liberal wing of the Democratic party—look upon insurance lobbyists as symbols of the powerful and sinister business lobby. A position taken by an insurance lobbyist, therefore, is likely to be related to the liberal ideological disposition of those legislators in a negative way. Thus, it is difficult for insurance lobbyists in Massachusetts to keep their position ''private,'' to maintain a degree of anonymity and detachment from ideological positions.

Using the "Soft Sell"

The desirability of keeping a position as noncontroversial as possible creates some curious complications with respect to perceptions of a lobbyist's power. It frequently happens that lobbyists are able to achieve a substantial portion of their goals without really being perceived as exerting much influence. This is especially true of business lobbyists, and most of the lobbyists at the state legislatures do represent private enterprise. While in Massachusetts only 34 percent of the lobbyists represent businesses, 81 percent of the North Carolina lobbyists, 65 percent of the Oregon lobbyists, and 51 percent of the Utah lobbyists represent businesses.[12]

Business lobbyists are inclined to define their role as one of stopping ''bad bills'' rather than of pushing for the passage of ''good bills''; but a clearer definition of their role perception can be found once again in the concept of persuasive versus informational communication. Business lobbyists do not appear as oriented toward the persuasive role as do lobbyists for labor unions and other types of organizations. Although it is technically easier to defeat legislation than to cause the passage of legislation, the true advantage of a nonpersuasive stance is that it enables the lobbyist to avoid purely persuasive communications. Business lobbyists are able to do

---

[12] For supportive evidence from other states, see Harmon Zeigler, ''Interest Groups in the States,'' in Herbert Jacob and Kenneth N. Vines, eds., *Politics in the American States* (Boston: Little, Brown and Co., 1965), p. 110.

this quite well. In all four states, labor lobbyists view their role as more persuasive than do business lobbyists. As a partial consequence of this perceived necessity to appear more persuasive in their communications, labor lobbyists seem to have made the task of lobbying somewhat more difficult for themselves. We have observed previously the positive relationships between direct lobbying and effectiveness and interaction and effectiveness. A singular exception to this rule is the labor lobbyists. In each state except North Carolina (where labor has scant representation), labor lobbyists score higher on the measure of interaction than do business lobbyists. Further, in two states, Oregon and Utah, labor lobbyists are more likely than business lobbyists to rely upon direct lobbying. Lastly, labor lobbyists in all four states rate themselves higher on the index of persuasion than do business lobbyists.

Given all these indications of effectiveness, the self-perceptions of labor lobbyists do not appear to be as optimistic as one would expect. When asked to evaluate their influence in comparison with other organizations, the representatives of labor are inclined to believe that they are less effective. In Oregon, for example, 58 percent of the labor lobbyists believe they have less success than other lobbyists, compared to 46 percent of the business lobbyists. In Utah, the percentages are 71 percent and 44 percent, respectively. The exception is Massachusetts, where 31 percent of the labor lobbyists rate themselves as less effective, compared to 56 percent of the business lobbyists. Thus, although labor lobbyists see themselves as achieving results, they see others as achieving even more results. Legislators and lobbyists alike tend to look upon labor as active and powerful, but the labor lobbyists themselves tend to reject this evaluation. This relatively self-denigrating self-perception is related not so much to an inability to rely upon defensive lobbying techniques as to the difficulty of developing a satisfactory interaction with a legislator when persuasion is perceived as a necessity.

Characteristics of Effective Lobbyists

As has been suggested, the "hard-sell" component of a lobbyist's communication is reduced when the initiative in communication is taken by the legislators. If a lobbyist can establish himself as someone to be sought out, the bias against the lobbying role is not as severe a problem. How does a lobbyist achieve this enviable position? What is it about some lobbyists that makes them appear desirable to legislators as sources of information? Is it because they are believed to be honest and knowledgeable? Perhaps this is one reason, but there is evidence to indicate also that those lobbyists who hold their jobs longest are those most likely to find themselves in demand as a source of information. In other words, simply "being around" helps quite a bit.

In Table 6.11, lobbyists are categorized into those with minimum experience (less than 2 years), moderate experience (between 3 and 10 years), high experience (between 11 and 25 years), and maximum experience (25 years or more). Plotted against these categorizations are the number of times per month the lobbyist is sought out by a legislator for his views on pending legislation. With the single exception of Massachusetts, the relationship between length of time lobbying and frequency of solicitation of views is positive. The longer one has been lobbying the greater the likelihood of interaction initiated by a legislator. The secret of success seems to be visibility. If a lobbyist is known as being the spokesman for a given interest, legislators will not have to spend time wondering whom they should contact for information pertaining to that interest. As the table indicates, the process of becoming known is a slow and arduous one. Given the importance of legislator-initiated communications, however, there is clearly no substitute for experience.

Although lobbyists as a group have greater occupational longevity than legislators, it is nevertheless true that relatively few individual lobbyists stay on the job long enough to become accepted sources of information. Curiously, the Oregon lobbyists are the least experienced group. The mean experience of the Oregon lobbyists is least of any state and there are more lobbyists in Oregon with less than two years of experience than in any other state. Indeed, Oregon is the only state in which the difference in the experience of legislators and lobbyists is insignificant. In view of the relationship between experience and frequency of solicitation, how is it possible that the Oregon amateurs are able to wield so much influence? The answer seems to be that, although the relationship between experience and frequency of solicitation of views holds in Oregon as well as in the other states, *all* Oregon lobbyists are called upon more frequently than are *any* lobbyists in any of the other states.

TABLE 6.11
Length of Time Lobbying and Frequency of Solicitation of Views

FREQUENCY OF SOLICITATION

Experience	Massachusetts				North Carolina				Oregon				Utah			
	1*	2	3	(N)	1	2	3	(N)	1	2	3	(N)	1	2	3	(N)
Low	75%	19	6	(32)	45%	45	10	(20)	28%	58	13	(53)	44%	25	31	(16)
2	67%	31	2	(88)	22%	63	15	(41)	13%	63	24	(67)	25%	58	18	(57)
3	54%	41	5	(39)	27%	58	15	(48)	12%	49	40	(43)	15%	50	35	(40)
High	82%	9	9	(11)	6%	63	31	(16)	0%	57	43	(7)	18%	59	24	(17)

* 1 = less than once a month

2 = 1 to 10 times a month

3 = more than 10 times a month

("Don't know's" and "no answer" categories are excluded.)

⌜In Oregon, then, interest groups are so firmly established as a source of information that the individual characteristics of lobbyists appear to be of little importance. This should not be taken to mean that Oregon legislators turn first to lobbyists when seeking information; as we have seen (Table 6.6), this does not happen in any state. Yet it does appear that the institutionalization of lobbying is strong enough in Oregon virtually to guarantee even an inexperienced lobbyist the opportunity to function as the target of communications as well as the initiator of communications. Lobbyists get into the game quicker in Oregon than in the other states and—not surprisingly—have a higher estimation of their success. Oregon lobbyists stand in striking contrast to Massachusetts lobbyists. More lobbyists at all levels of experience are contacted by legislators in Oregon than in Massachusetts. The most experienced Massachusetts lobbyists do not enjoy positions any more favorable in this respect than the novices. Thus, while the legislative system of the strong-lobby states (as typified by Oregon) incorporates lobbyists into the consultative process very early in their careers, the legislative system of the weak-lobby states (as typified by Massachusetts) tends to exclude lobbyists from the consultative process whatever their experience.⌟

In a previous chapter, we discussed the frequency with which lobbyists are called upon by legislators to perform influence services (influencing other legislators, helping to amass public opinion, and participation in planning strategy) and information services (communicating with other lobbyists and researching a particular bill). We pointed out the tendency of lobbyists to emphasize influence services and the contrasting tendency of legislators to emphasize informational services, and noted that this casts some doubt upon the degree to which either set of responses can be interpreted as descriptive of reality. However, it is possible to use these responses to illustrate further the contrast between inexperienced and experienced lobbyists in strong- and weak-lobby states.

Since we are dealing only with the responses of the lobbyists in this case, perhaps a word of caution should be issued with regard to the responses of North Carolina lobbyists. It will be recalled that the greatest discrepancy between the responses of legislators and the responses of lobbyists was found in North Carolina. In the other states, lobbyists' responses were found to be fairly close to the perceptions of legislators. Thus, though we cannot give full credence to the responses from North Carolina, we can give credence to our finding that experience counts for very little in Massachusetts. If we select one example from informational services (performing research) and another example from influence services (participation in planning strategy), we find that in neither case does the acquisition of experience really benefit the Massachusetts lobbyist (see Table 6.12). Again disregarding the responses of North Carolina lobbyists, we note that the novices in Oregon and Utah are

TABLE 6.12

Length of Time Lobbying and Utilization of Skills for Information and Influence Services: Percentages of Lobbyists Called upon "Frequently" or "Occasionally" to Research a Bill or Participate in Planning Strategy

	Massachusetts		North Carolina		Oregon		Utah	
Experience	Re-search	Plan-ning	Re-search	Plan-ning	Re-search	Plan-ning	Re-search	Plan-ning
Low	41%	35%	60%	45%	59%	50%	56%	63%
2	43	32	85	77	79	72	65	75
3	46	48	72	66	80	60	64	78
High	36	36	77	82	100	71	65	71

likely to be called upon for both influence and informational services substantially more often than are the most experienced lobbyists in Massachusetts.

If one were searching for a universal trait which characterized the effective lobbyist, therefore, he would have to impose qualifications upon the characteristic of experience. Apparently the difficulties of the Massachusetts lobbyists are so great that even those with considerable experience do not enjoy a favorable position. What characteristic, then, does contribute to success, irrespective of the political system in which the lobbying takes place? We observed earlier that two essential characteristics of the effective lobbyists are perceived integrity and perceived expertise. Presumably, integrity is a characteristic which is not related to any other specific characteristic of the lobbyist. That is to say, whether or not a lobbyist is experienced or inexperienced is not automatically associated with integrity. There is, as we would expect, a clearer relationship between length of time lobbying and perceptions of expertise. Still, given the deviant case of Massachusetts, this relationship also is not absolute.

Other characteristics of lobbyists have been popularly assumed to contribute to effectiveness. One of these is legal training. Can we assume that lobbyists who are lawyers are more effective than lobbyists who are nonlawyers because the possession of legal skills can be translated into legislative skills? The only study which explicitly tests the relationship between occupation and effectiveness is DeVries' study of the Michigan lobbyist. DeVries found no relationship between legal training and lobbyists' effectiveness.[13] The data here suggests that DeVries' conclusions are generalizable beyond Michigan. In general, lobbyists who are lawyers are not more effective than lobbyists who are not.

Another possible candidate for a universal characteristic of effective lobbyists is that of previous governmental experience. One might suppose that interest groups would be anxious to employ people who had previous experience, because such experience might increase the lobbyist's knowledge of the legislative process. However, relatively few ex-legislators ever become lobbyists. Zeller, Patterson, Epstein, and DeVries have called attention to the absence of ex-legislators among lobbyists.[14] As we noted in Chapter 3, the situation in four states under consideration here supports these findings. Only a small fraction of the lobbyists in these states have served in the state legislatures. On the other hand, quite a few lobbyists have had other forms of governmental experience. Whether people with governmental experience are sought out by interest groups or whether there is a natural tendency of such people to drift back into political activity is not known. However, if interest groups are anxious to employ effective lobbyists, they would be wise to look for those with previous governmental experience, because the evidence suggests that these lobbyists are more likely to be sought out by legislators than are lobbyists who have not enjoyed the benefits of this experience.

[13] Walter DeVries, ''The Michigan Lobbyist: A Study in the Bases and Perceptions of Effectiveness'' (Ph.D. dissertation, Michigan State University, 1960).

[14] Belle Zeller, ed., *American State Legislatures* (New York: Thomas Y. Crowell Co., 1954), p. 249; Samuel C. Patterson, ''The Role of the Lobbyist: The Case of Oklahoma,'' *Journal of Politics*, 25 (1963), 76; DeVries, p. 78; Leon Epstein, *Politics in Wisconsin* (Madison, Wisc.: University of Wisconsin Press, 1958), pp. 118–119.

Returning now to our analysis of informational and influence activities, we note that for both types of services, lobbyists with previous governmental experience are in greater demand (see Table 6.13). This is true even in Massachusetts, where, as we have seen, experience is not related to legislator-initiated communication. It is true, of course, that those lobbyists who have held previous governmental positions in Massachusetts are sought out substantially less frequently than are lobbyists of comparable previous

TABLE 6.13

Governmental Experience of Lobbyists and Solicitation of Their Services by Legislators: Percentages "Frequently" or "Occasionally" Called upon to Research Bills or Participate in Planning Strategy

	Massa-chusetts (N)	North Carolina (N)	Oregon (N)	Utah (N)
RESEARCH A BILL				
Previous governmental experience	55% (60)	74% (80)	82% (76)	68% (68)
No governmental experience	38 (125)	67 (52)	67 (117)	58 (66)
PARTICIPATE IN PLANNING STRATEGY				
Previous governmental experience	40	75	64	81
No governmental experience	35	69	61	65

experience in other states. Nevertheless, since Massachusetts lobbyists with governmental experience are sought out more than Massachusetts lobbyists without governmental experience, it is suggested that such experience is at least one essential characteristic of the effective lobbyist. However, even here a note of caution should be introduced. DeVries found no significant relationship between nonlegislative governmental experience and lobbying effectiveness. He found only that those lobbyists with legislative experience are more effective. The data reported here suggests that any governmental experience is helpful. Whether or not such experience tangibly contributes to expertise, legislators apparently believe it does.

Styles of Business and Labor Lobbyists

Not all types of services are performed equally by all lobbyists. We noted in an earlier chapter that lobbyists are inclined to emphasize their influence services over their informational ones, and speculated that this emphasis is in keeping with the lobbyist's image of himself as a manipulator. We also observed that labor lobbyists, who are usually identified as using pressure techniques, are also generally more active in the lobbying process and are more likely to define their role as persuasive.

If we examine the performance of influence and informational services by business and labor lobbyists, we find that the behavior of both groups reflects their images of themselves (see Table 6.14). It

TABLE 6.14

Percentages of Business and Labor Lobbyists Called
upon to Perform Influence and Informational Services*

	Massachusetts (N)		Oregon (N)		Utah (N)	
INFLUENCE LEGISLATORS						
Business	12%	(50)	51%	(98)	61%	(54)
Labor	54	(13)	64	(33)	93	(14)
COMMUNICATE WITH OTHER LOBBYISTS						
Business	22		47		65	
Labor	77		64		93	
AMASS PUBLIC OPINION						
Business	28		36		57	
Labor	69		61		86	
CONDUCT RESEARCH						
Business	50		79		69	
Labor	54		51		71	
PARTICIPATE IN PLANNING STRATEGY						
Business	30		72		72	
Labor	54		73		79	

* North Carolina excluded because of lack of labor lobbyists.

can be seen that in most cases labor lobbyists perform services for legislators more frequently than do business lobbyists. This is especially true of activities which might be defined as "lobbying" in the popularly understood sense of the word. For example, labor lobbyists are substantially more likely to be called upon to try to influence other legislators than are business lobbyists. Indeed, in Massachusetts, where lobbyists are generally so inactive, the labor lobbyists appear to get into the act quite a lot.

We have already described the process whereby a lobbyist will use a legislator as an intermediary. Here we see that the reverse process often occurs; legislators often call upon lobbyists to intercede with other legislators. The labor lobbyist seems to dominate this process. He also dominates the process of finding out for a legislator how other lobbyists stand on an issue. Much of the information supplied by any lobbyist is, in fact, of this nose-counting variety. Many times legislators who do not use lobbyists for technical information will go to them for information about the general division of opinion on legislation. It appears, once more, that labor lobbyists are most qualified to perform this task.

If legislators wish to drum up public support for their position, they again seem to find labor lobbyists particularly helpful. Massachusetts labor lobbyists perform this function more often than do Oregon labor lobbyists, and this is one of the few examples of greater activity on the part of the Massachusetts lobbyist. However, while business lobbyists seem to be less likely to involve themselves in the transmission to legislators of information about lobbyists, other legislators, or the general public, they do participate quite frequently in less spectacular activities, such as conducting research. In this case the difference between the activities of business and labor lobbyists is slight; in one state (Oregon), actually, business lobbyists perform this service more than do the labor lobbyists. It is also true that, unlike labor lobbyists, business lobbyists are more likely to participate in planning strategy than they are in other activities. It seems, therefore, that the lobbying styles of business and labor lobbyists are not at all similar. Labor lobbyists are more aggressive and persuasive, and thus elect to devote their time largely to the exchange of influence and of political, rather than technical, information. Business lobbyists, who are generally less active in the overall interaction process, see their role as more informational than influential, and thus concentrate their energies upon information and the quieter aspects of strategy making. The more "informational" activity of business lobbyists might reflect the fact that business interest groups tend to recruit former government officials, men valued for their possession of information. Forty-eight percent of the business lobbyists have previous governmental experience, compared to 25 percent of the labor lobbyists.

Do Lobbyists Concentrate on the Leadership?

An important factor in examining services performed by lobbyists and indeed in examining any interaction between legislators and lobbyists, is the kind of legislator who is making the request or the kind of legislator whom most lobbyists wish to see. One of the bothersome aspects of relying as heavily as we do on the concept of interaction is that that concept fails to take into account the possibility that most legislators are not really important to lobbyists. In a state in which decision making is heavily concentrated in the hands of the leadership, lobbyists would be ill-advised to spend much time talking to ordinary members. Since Massachusetts is such a state, one might argue that the mere fact that the average member of the legislature sees very little of lobbyists does not necessarily mean that the impact of lobbyists upon legislative decision making is minimal. If, in Massachusetts, the Speaker and other leaders are more likely to interact with lobbyists than are the average members, then perhaps the failure of lobbyists to interact with many legislators is not a reflection of their importance to legislators but rather a reflection of sound strategy on their part.

The data lend some support to such an argument. Of all the states under consideration here, only in Massachusetts do leaders (including committee chairmen) have more interaction with lobbyists than do nonleaders. In North Carolina, nonleaders have more interaction than leaders; in Oregon and Utah, the rates of interaction are virtually identical. In Massachusetts, 47 percent of the leaders have less than five contacts per week with lobbyists compared to 69 percent of the nonleaders. Forty-five percent of the leaders have between six and twenty-five weekly contacts compared to 27 percent of the nonleaders, and 7 percent of the leaders have more than twenty-six contacts per week compared to 4 percent of the nonleaders. There is some justification, therefore, in maintaining that the generally low rate of interaction between legislators and lobbyists in Massachusetts is dictated by strategy. In a highly institutionalized system in which the leadership's power is immense, as it is in Massachusetts, the average legislator is not really a suitable target for lobbyists. However, it is important to notice that even the leaders of the Massachusetts legislature have substantially less interaction with lobbyists than do the legislators of other states. For example, 55 percent of the legislative leaders in Oregon interact at a rate of twenty-six times or more per week, compared to 7 percent of the Massachusetts legislative leaders. Therefore, even those legislators who are the most likely targets for Massachusetts lobbyists do not see as much of them as do legislators in other states. This is not to say that Massachusetts lobbyists do not try to see the leadership as actively as lobbyists in other states try to see legislators in general. The fact is that the leadership in Massachusetts has carefully insulated itself against lobbyists. For example, the Speaker of the House employs an administrative assistant whose job is primarily to keep lobbyists away. This assistant boasts that 75 percent of the lobbyists who try to see the Speaker are unsuccessful. In no other state has the leadership taken such pains to insulate itself from lobbyists.

7 THE
EFFECTS
OF
LOBBYING

In this chapter, we wish to assess the over-all impact of interest groups on the legislative decision-making process. We have estimated the persuasive effects of various techniques of lobbying, but we have yet to consider the total contribution of lobbyists to the informational matrix of the legislature. If lobbyists were suddenly to disappear, would it really make any difference?

Rates of Interaction

If they are to be effective, lobbyists have to interact with legislators frequently and on a regularized basis. Therefore, an analysis of interest-group strength must begin with an assessment of the frequency of lobbyist-legislator interaction. In order to make such an assessment, we asked legislators and lobbyists how many contacts (of any kind) per week occurred between them during the legislative session.[1] The results are reported in Table 7.1. The table indicates substantial interstate differences. More frequent contact is reported by both legislators and lobbyists in Oregon than by either group in any other state. The least frequent interactions are reported by legislators and lobbyists in Massachusetts. Utah falls between the two extremes. North

[1] It would obviously have been better to *observe* the number of interactions than to ask the participants to recall them, but to do so would have been impossible both in terms of comparative research and in terms of time involved. The table should be interpreted as an estimate.

146

Carolina, however, is more difficult to classify. In each of the other states, legislators and lobbyists are relatively close in their assessments of the frequency of interaction, but, in North Carolina, legislators think little interaction takes place, while lobbyists would

TABLE 7.1

Mean Interactions Per Week

	Mean	(N)
MASSACHUSETTS		
Legislators	7.8	(244)
Lobbyists	10.7	(185)
NORTH CAROLINA		
Legislators	8.5	(164)
Lobbyists	25.9	(132)
OREGON		
Legislators	34.0	(84)
Lobbyists	31.0	(193)
UTAH		
Legislators	16.0	(90)
Lobbyists	18.5	(134)

"rank" their state second only to Oregon in this respect. Here we encounter a basic problem in Eulau's suggestion that both participants in an interaction should be examined. If those participants radically disagree in their accounts of the interaction, which of them is right? One possibility, of course, as McAdams has suggested in another context, is that lobbyists tend to exaggerate their importance to legislators, while legislators, conforming to their idea of a good legislator, like to believe they are acting "independently."[2] This explanation, however, has the obvious flaw of failing to account for the tendency of legislators in other states to approximate the estimates of lobbyists. Oregon legislators, in fact, actually see *more* interaction than do lobbyists.

Still, there may be some truth in the explanation in the specific case of North Carolina. North Carolina is less urban, less industrialized, and less wealthy than the other states. It also has the lowest rate of public political participation. These conditions generally contribute to the strength of an interest-group system, but at the

[2] Alan K. McAdams, *Power and Politics in Labor Legislation* (New York: Columbia University Press, 1964), p. 193.

same time might contribute to the reluctance of legislators to discuss interest groups, or to the failure of legislators to be able to offer accurate assessments of the effect of interest-group activities. Furthermore, North Carolina has, according to Elazar, a traditionalistic political culture. The essential attribute of such a culture is ''a paternalistic and elitist concept of the commonwealth.'' Consequently, such a culture confines ''real political power to a relatively small and self-perpetuating group drawn from an established elite,'' an elite comprised of persons considered to have a ''right'' to govern.[3] If legislators reflect this kind of attitude, they would admit very little ''outside'' influence, whether from party, interest group, or constituents. Wahlke and his associates came to much the same conclusion when evaluating the politics of Tennessee—a state with essentially the same kind of political culture as North Carolina. There are more ''trustees'' to be found in Tennessee than in any of the other states examined by Wahlke and his colleagues.[4] A trustee defines his legislative role as that of a free agent, one who relies on his own conscience and principles rather than on the advice of any external source. Therefore, trustees would be reluctant to place much reliance on lobbyists, or, perhaps, to *admit* that they do so.

The fact that interest groups seem to play such a minor role in the Massachusetts legislative system might, in part, be a result of the strong party cohesion in that legislature. Moreover, Massachusetts is a populous, ethnically diverse state, and this, on the one hand, might produce more demands for legislative action, but, on the other hand, might also increase the number of competitors for rewards (still, there are fewer registered lobbyists in Massachusetts than in Oregon). Massachusetts also has nearly three times as many legislators as does either Oregon or Utah, making the task of interaction difficult purely on the basis of the ratio of legislators to lobbyists.[5] Interaction might also be affected by the size of the

---

[3] Daniel Elazar, *American Federalism: A View From the States* (New York: Thomas Y. Crowell Co., 1966), p. 93.

[4] John C. Wahlke, Heinz Eulau, William Buchanan, LeRoy C. Ferguson, *The Legislative System* (New York: John Wiley, 1961), p. 281.

[5] The idea that the difficulty of the lobbyist's job is related to the size of the audience can be explored by examining the interaction rates of the state senates, which have fewer members. In Massachusetts and Utah there is substantially more interaction in the Senate than in the House. However, in North Carolina, there is substantially less contact in the Senate, while in Oregon the interaction rates are virtually the same.

capital city, and Boston is a large city in which legislators can be hard to find. Salem, Oregon, on the other hand, is a small town in which the legislature is the main focal point of activity. Salt Lake City, between Boston and Salem in population, is the seat of a legislature which also yields an interaction rate between the two extremes of Massachusetts and Oregon. Of course, one can hardly maintain that the size of the capital city *per se* is a basic contributor to the rate of interaction. However, in Massachusetts, at any rate, the job of the lobbyist, already made difficult by the limited visibility of interest groups in that state (compared to the state's strong political parties), might be further complicated by the size of the capital city. The weakness of interest groups in North Carolina and Massachusetts appears easier to explain than the strength of interest groups in Oregon and Utah. As the argument of this chapter develops, attempts will be made to correct this deficiency.

The fact that legislators and lobbyists have different perceptions of the extent of communication might be indicative of variations among the states in patterns of interaction. Both sets of judges might be correct. In a state in which legislators perceive more communication than do lobbyists, for example, we might find that the bulk of interaction occurs between a few lobbyists and a great many legislators. In other words, the target of lobbyists' communications might be quite large in comparison to the number of lobbyists attempting to communicate. The best examples of this possibility are Oregon and Utah. The larger targets of lobbyists in these states may reflect the relatively open decision-making structure of their legislatures. Neither strong parties nor traditionalistic cultures would restrict the number of legislators in Oregon and Utah who might be viewed as useful targets for communication. The strategy of the lobbyist in these states would, thus, be to contact as many legislators as possible, whether or not they hold important party or legislative positions. Yet, since a relatively small proportion of Oregon or Utah lobbyists are full-time "professionals," this relatively large body of target legislators would interact with a far smaller number of lobbyists. This number would be proportionally somewhat larger in Oregon than in Utah, however, since Oregon has a higher proportion of "professional" lobbyists.

Two contrasting patterns are presented by North Carolina and Massachusetts, neither of which have broad target areas. In Massachusetts, few lobbyists interact with few legislators. In North Carolina, many lobbyists interact with few legislators. The rigidity of party control in Massachusetts may well eliminate the rank-and-file legislator in that state from the communication process, while the traditionalism and the value placed upon experience in North Carolina may do the same thing there. In North Carolina, however, the case for a restricted target zone appears strengthened because of the greater activity of lobbyists. North Carolina brings to mind the research of Garceau and Silverman,[6] which suggests that many Vermont legislators are unaware of intense lobbying activity, and of Wahlke, Eulau, Buchanan, and Ferguson, who find Tennessee legislators similarly unaware, but draw a different conclusion: that in Tennessee not much lobbying takes place. In the case of North Carolina, it is true that most legislators are not involved in the lobbying process, but this does not necessarily mean that little lobbying takes place.

Another approach to the problem of legislators' and lobbyists' differing perceptions of interaction is to find out what *kinds* of lobbyists and legislators are most likely to interact. It may be, for instance, that interaction increases with the experience of either the legislator or the lobbyist or both. In the case of lobbyists, it may take time to locate key decision makers, become familiar with the rules of the game, learn the technicalities of legislation, establish a reputation, and get on friendly terms with legislators. Legislators, for their part, might have increased contact with lobbyists if their positions in the legislature have become sufficiently important to attract the attention of lobbyists. Since turnover in the ranks of both groups is fairly high, perhaps only a minority of either group really gets involved in interaction.

To some extent, these speculations are supported by the data, but not in a clear fashion. In all states except Utah, the experienced lobbyists do have a higher rate of interaction with legislators than do the novices. In Utah, the novice lobbyists actually have more contacts with legislators than do the experienced ones. Assuming that the experienced lobbyists know more about their jobs, this suggests that Utah lobbyists have found that limiting contact is good strategy. Both North Carolina (52 percent) and Utah (44 percent) have a higher proportion of experienced lobbyists than Oregon (30 percent) and Massachusetts (29 percent).[7] However, in

[6] Oliver Garceau and Corinne Silverman, "A Pressure Group and the Pressured: A Case Report," *American Political Science Review,* 43 (September 1954), 672–691.

[7] The cut-point for experience is eleven years.

spite of the similarity in the amount of experience of their lobbyists, there are marked differences between each member of each
pair of states with respect to intensity of interaction.

A similar pattern emerges for legislators; except in North Carolina, those legislators with the most experience have the greatest
contact with lobbyists. The case of North Carolina is puzzling. We
have described North Carolina as a relatively "closed" state in
which only the more experienced lobbyists actually get into the act
of contacting a few legislators. But the experienced legislators do
not absorb the bulk of the efforts of lobbyists, as they do in other
states. Nor do committee chairmen or party leaders receive more
communications from lobbyists than do nonleaders, as they do in
other states. The structure of power in North Carolina's legislature,
then—insofar as it can be ascertained from the efforts of lobbyists
—is totally unrelated to the formal structure of the institution.

On the basis of interaction—without concern for the *effects* of
interaction—Oregon and Massachusetts stand at opposite ends of a
continuum, with North Carolina (depending upon the judges) and
Utah falling in between. Of course, interaction need not be an
indicator of effect. Perhaps one contact by a good lobbyist is worth a
hundred contacts by an amateur. Also, perhaps the greater the
number of contacts—indicating a more intense set of demands—the
less effective any one contact is likely to be. Further, intensity of
interaction might simply be a function of how busy legislators are.
The more bills there are to consider, the more frequent will be the
interaction (assuming that interest groups are the basic communicator of demands). This last hypothesis, however, clearly does not
work, because Massachusetts, with its low rate of interaction, considers almost twice as many bills per day (19) as does Oregon
(10).

Although the explanation of the reasons for varied rates of
interaction is parted at this point, let us proceed to the next step in
the argument. The question is: to what extent does frequency of
interaction provide clues about the effects of the interaction?

Effects of Lobbying

Measuring the effects of lobbying is especially difficult in view of
the contrasting perceptions of legislators and lobbyists and because
of the existence of at least two functions of lobbying. If lobbying is

persuasive, we need to know how often this goal is achieved. If lobbying is informational, we need to know how much confidence is placed in the information. The point is that a single measure of influence is not able to account for the *ends* attached to various lobbying *means*.

Mention was made earlier of the report by Zeller.[8] Political scientists were asked to describe the influence of interest groups in their states as "strong," "moderate," or "weak." The defects of this method are apparent. The panel of judges is, at best, questionable. Asking people to evaluate the effects of interest groups in terms of such an ambiguous concept as "power" compounds the felony. A better method was devised by Wahlke, Eulau, Buchanan, and Ferguson. Their measure was based on questions dealing with both the legislators' awareness of interest groups and their acceptance of the legitimacy of lobbying. By combining legislators' attitudes (as measured by a series of scales) and awareness (as measured by ability to identify certain organizations), legislators were classified into three role-orientations: facilitators, neutrals, and resisters. Thus, in no case was anybody asked simply about the power of interest groups. However, as we noted earlier, there are some problems with this scheme. The classifications are only minimally behavioral. They deal not with actions but only with attitudes. Wahlke reasons that legislators can be expected to behave according to their role definitions and that the behavioral consequences follow naturally from role definitions. Our data do indicate, in support of Wahlke, that the extent of contact, effect of contact, and attitudes of legislators toward lobbyists are clearly interrelated. However, our data also challenge one of Wahlke's conclusions, that percentage of resisters declines as legislative experience increases. We found that, whereas the *attitudes* of legislators toward lobbyists do become more favorable as experience increases, legislators *do not* become more persuadable. A consequence of this lack of connection between behavior and attitude is that Wahlke's discussion of interest-group politics is a discussion of potential, a discussion which avoids an account of what happens in favor of an estimate of what might happen. In the end, the distinction between potential and actuality is lost.

There is no clear way out of these dilemmas, but our approach is to consider lobbying as both a persuasive and informational process

[8] Belle Zeller, ed., *American State Legislatures* (New York: Thomas Y. Crowell Co., 1954), pp. 190–191.

and to assess the effects of both attempts, relying upon reports of behavior more than upon assessment of attitudes.[9]

We might begin by observing some apparent differences between lobbying in the states and lobbying in Washington. In Washington, where lobbying is typically informational, lobbyists talk almost exclusively to sympathetic legislators. In the states, where lobbying is more often persuasive, opponents seem to have considerably more contact with each other. It is true that more contact takes place among like-minded lobbyists and legislators than among those who do not see things in the same way, but in all states at least a third of the legislators and lobbyists also indicate substantial contact with opponents. In Oregon, to cite a slightly atypical case, about the same number of contacts take place between those with conflicting points of view as between those in agreement.[10] In short, lobbyists in the states appear to "lobby" in the traditional, stereotypic sense more than do lobbyists in Washington. Younger state lobbyists are more likely to conform to the stereotype than older ones. That is, the younger lobbyist is more likely to talk to opponents and to define his role as that of a persuader. There is a sort of professionalization process which reduces the stereotypic behavior of lobbyists as they begin to learn the rules of the game. This process is certainly related to number of interactions. The greater the number of interactions, the more realistic become the participants' images of each other. Hence, younger lobbyists, who have not been "in the game" very long, have not had the opportunity to correct their stereotypes.

Another aspect of stereotypic behavior which is probably related to extent of interaction concerns the notion of "pressure." To legislators and lobbyists, "pressure" has an undesirable connotation. When a legislator says that he is being pressured, he means that he perceives the lobbyist to be trying vigorously to overcome his resistance by any available means.

The perceived incidence of pressure varies from state to state and between legislators and lobbyists. Massachusetts lobbyists, who report very little contact with legislators, are far more likely to

---

[9] Since this analysis is based upon reports of behavior rather than independent observations of behavior, the point of our objection to Wahlke's approach is questionable. Nevertheless, in using reports as a surrogate for behavior, the effort to describe behavior is clear.

[10] *Most* of the Oregon lobbyist's contacts, however, are with "neutral" legislators, legislators whose positions are unclear.

believe themselves to engage in pressure tactics than are lobbyists in the other states. In Massachusetts, as is true in the other states, legislators tend to see less pressure than lobbyists. The discrepancy between the perceptions of the two sets of judges is substantially greater in this case than in the case of any other state (see Chapter 6).

By contrast, Oregon, which appears to have the greatest amount of interaction, also appears to have the lowest perception of pressure tactics on the parts of both legislators and lobbyists. The general rule seems to be that interaction and perceptions of pressure exist in a functional relationship. The greater the interaction between legislators and lobbyists, the more favorable become the legislators' evaluations of the encounter. The exception is Utah, where there is both a high interaction rate and a high perception of pressure. Indeed, Utah legislators believe themselves to be more pressured than the legislators of any other state. As will become evident shortly, although Utah and Oregon seem to be the two states in which interest groups are most active, the attitudes toward lobbyists of legislators in these states is quite different. There is a general reluctance on the part of legislators in Utah to accept interest groups as legitimate, even though they come into frequent contact with them. It can be demonstrated that, whereas interaction occurs only slightly less frequently in Utah than in Oregon, the effects of interaction are considerably less in Utah than in Oregon.

As a measure of the effectiveness of lobbying, we tabulated the responses of legislators to three questions based upon the assumptions of Guttman scaling.[11] Legislators were asked, first, whether they could recall being influenced by a lobbyist to the point of questioning their position about any given issue. Next, they were asked if they could recall being influenced by a lobbyist to the extent of changing their opinion on an issue so that it was not as far from the position of the lobbyist as it was initially. Finally, legisla-

---

[11] Guttman scaling assumes that if a respondent has performed the most extreme act in a sequence of related acts, he has also performed the less extreme acts. In this case, if a legislator says he has been converted to the position of the lobbyist, we would expect him also to have been influenced to lean more toward the position of the lobbyist and to have questioned his own position on an issue. If the legislator says he has been converted but also says he has not questioned his position on an issue, he has given a response that cannot be properly scaled.

A second assumption of Guttman scaling is described in the text.

tors were asked if they could recall being influenced to the extent of reaching total agreement with the position of the lobbyist. Thus, the first question represents minimum effect and the last question represents maximum effect. Lobbyists were also asked these questions, with appropriate modifications in wording.

Guttman scaling assumes that the frequency of the successful performance of a task will decrease with the difficulty of the task. This assumption held true for lobbyists. According to lobbyists, they are able to produce "questioning" and "leaning" responses more often than they are able to produce a "conversion" (see Table 7.2). With legislators, however, the assumption does not hold true in all cases. In both Oregon and Utah, legislators indicate that they have changed positions more often than they have undergone more moderate forms of persuasion.

Table 7.2 confirms what we have learned so far about the four states under examination. Massachusetts lobbyists are far more skeptical about their ability to achieve successful results than are the lobbyists in any other state. This pessimism is shared to some extent by legislators. The gap between the perceptions of legislators

TABLE 7.2

Extent of Influence: Percentages of Legislators and Lobbyists Believing Legislators Have Been "Frequently" or "Occasionally" Influenced

| | Extent of Influence | | | |
	Questioning a previously held opinion	Leaning more toward the views of the lobbyist	Changing from one position to another	(N)
MASSACHUSETTS				
Legislators	34%	31	20	(244)
Lobbyists	51%	39	26	(185)
NORTH CAROLINA				
Legislators	22%	20	18	(164)
Lobbyists	76%	70	39	(132)
OREGON				
Legislators	45%	42	51	(84)
Lobbyists	79%	52	41	(193)
UTAH				
Legislators	32%	38	42	(90)
Lobbyists	77%	66	48	(134)

and the perceptions of lobbyists is far less severe in Massachusetts than in North Carolina. North Carolina lobbyists see their influence as far greater than do legislators. Indeed, the North Carolina lobbyists (whose legislators consider them impotent) have almost as high an estimation of the success of their efforts as do the Oregon lobbyists (whose legislators consider them powerful), and in one category ("leaning") the North Carolina lobbyists appear to be more optimistic. The table also adds weight to the argument that Oregon and Utah are strong-lobby states, whereas Massachusetts and North Carolina are weak-lobby states, especially when we consider the opinions of legislators.

Naturally, lobbyists, as a rule, exaggerate the impact of their efforts. However, there is one exception to this rule that deserves mention. In Oregon, more legislators than lobbyists believe that conversion has occurred. In this particular case, lobbyists are underestimating substantially the impact of their communications. The difference in the perceptions between legislators and lobbyists is least in Oregon and Massachusetts (see Table 7.3), with both sets

TABLE 7.3

Differences in Legislators' and Lobbyists' Perceptions of Extent of Influence

| | Extent of Influence | | | |
	Questioning a previously held position	Leaning more toward the views of the lobbyist	Changing from one position to another	Average
Massachusetts	−17*	− 8	− 6	−10
North Carolina	−54	−50	−21	−42
Oregon	−34	−10	+10	−15
Utah	−44	−28	− 6	−26

The differences between the percentages reported for the two groups of respondents in Table 7.2. Negative signs indicate a higher percentage of lobbyists reporting the effect; positive signs indicate a higher percentage of legislators reporting the effect.

of judges in Oregon agreeing that lobbyists are powerful and both in Massachusetts agreeing that lobbyists are ineffective. These sorts of realistic appraisals are, of course, not found in North Carolina or in Utah. The optimism of the Oregon lobbyists is earned, as is the pessimism of the Massachusetts lobbyists. To a lesser extent, the optimism of the Utah lobbyists is realistic, but the optimism of the North Carolina lobbyists is apparently without foundation.

Conversion does occur in the states more frequently than it seems to in Washington. We would expect legislators to underestimate the extent of conversion; but, even taking this into account, a slight majority of Oregon lawmakers and a large minority of Utah legislators indicated that they have been switched from one position to another by lobbyists. These data assume, of course, that the job of the lobbyist is to change minds. However, as we have seen, there are two role definitions of the job of the lobbyist: that of persuader and that of informant. Needless to say, these role definitions are not mutually exclusive; it is possible for lobbyists to perform different roles at different times or even simultaneously. Further, the data should not be interpreted to mean that more subtle, less explicit modes of communication cannot have a persuasive consequence.

This chapter is concerned not with lobbying strategies but with lobbying strengths. Nevertheless, one source of strength, and indeed perhaps a crucial source, is the extent to which legislators accept the lobbyist as a legitimate source of information. Our data indicate that, whereas there is no relationship between the amount of contact between legislators and lobbyists and the persuasibility of legislators, there is a clear and strong relationship between the extent of communication *initiated* by legislators and the degree of their persuasibility. The more often a legislator seeks out lobbyists, the more likely he is to be persuaded by them (see Table 7.4). Consequently, one source of the strength of interest groups in Oregon and Utah might be found in the fact that two thirds of the legislators in those states indicate that they solicit the opinions of lobbyists when an issue arises in which the lobbyists have legitimate interests. In contrast, only slightly more than one third of the legislators in Massachusetts and North Carolina seek out lobbyists in this (or any other) situation.

We might assume that the seeking out of lobbyists indicates an acceptance on the part of the legislators of the legitimacy of the place of interest groups in the legislative process. Thus, we would expect lobbyists to be accorded a higher degree of acceptance by legislators in the strong-lobby states than by legislators in the weak-lobby states. However, this does not hold true consistently for the four states of our study. By a variety of measures it appears, for example, that the attitude of Utah legislators toward lobbyists is far more hostile than their behavior would indicate. Consider, for example, a question we asked of legislators which approaches the legitimacy of lobbyists from a slightly different angle. Legislators were asked if they believed it proper to be seen socially with a lobbyist. Whereas 83 percent of the Oregon legislators indicated it

TABLE 7.4

Percentage* of Legislators Reporting Influence and
Extent of Interaction Initiated by the Legislator

Legislator-Initiated Interaction	Questioning a previously held opinion	Extent of Influence Leaning more toward the views of the lobbyist	Changing from one position to another	(N)***
MASSACHUSETTS				
Low**	28%	26	24	(156)
Medium	51%	42	44	(41)
High	47%	53	60	(15)
NORTH CAROLINA				
Low	19%	18	15	(130)
Medium	32%	32	23	(22)
High	38%	13	38	(8)
,OREGON				
Low	29%	33	42	(24)
Medium	63%	53	57	(30)
High	46%	50	63	(24)
UTAH				
Low	24%	32	44	(50)
Medium	39%	46	39	(26)
High	60%	50	50	(10)

* Percentage of legislators reporting that an event had occurred "frequently" or "occasionally."
** Low = less than 5 contacts per week.
Medium = 6–25 contacts per week.
High = 26 or more contacts per week.
*** "Don't know's" are excluded.

was proper to be seen with a lobbyist, only 68 percent of the Utah legislators indicated it was proper. Fewer Utah legislators are comfortable in the presence of lobbyists than Massachusetts legislators (75 percent), and Utah lobbyists are exceeded in their discomfort only by North Carolina legislators (58 percent). Thus, legislators in

one of the "strong-lobby states" are more circumspect in the presence of lobbyists than legislators in one of the "weak-lobby
states."

The peculiarities of Utah can be examined further by returning
to the problem of the relationship between attitudes and behavior.
There is a relationship between the two, but this relationship does
not emerge very clearly in Utah. For instance, there is no relationship in Utah between the attitudes of legislators toward interest
groups and the extent of interaction. Those legislators who have an
unfavorable attitude toward lobbyists are just about as likely to
interact with lobbyists as those who do not. A good illustration of
the Utah legislator's suspicion of the lobbying process can be seen in
Table 7.5, which presents the attitudes which legislators have to-

TABLE 7.5

Attitudes of Legislators toward Information Received from Lobbyists

	Depend upon information from lobbyists*	Have confidence in information from lobbyists**	Find information from lobbyists helpful***	(N)
Massachusetts	50%	55	41	(244)
North Carolina	41%	56	28	(164)
Oregon	83%	88	61	(84)
Utah	80%	70	43	(90)

* Percentage reporting they depend upon information from lobbyists "a good
deal" or "some" of the time.
** Percentage indicating they have "a lot" or "quite a bit" of confidence in
information from lobbyists.
*** Percentage indicating that "all" or "most" of the information is helpful.

ward the information they receive from lobbyists. It can be seen
that Utah legislators depend upon lobbyists for information almost
as much as do Oregon legislators, but that the confidence that Utah
legislators have in this information is substantially less. Moreover, a
substantially smaller percentage of Utah legislators, as compared to
Oregon legislators, even find information received from lobbyists
especially helpful. Indeed, they appear almost as unimpressed with
such information as the Massachusetts legislators. Thus, it is clear
that the dependence of Utah legislators upon the services of lobbyists is not based solely upon a facilitating attitude. It appears
that interaction between Utah lobbyists and legislators is not en-

tered into in a purely voluntary way. The interaction seems to be forced upon each actor. In the political arena there are compelling reasons for the continuing functioning of an interaction system in spite of private attitudes. Certain things have to be done: laws have to be passed, information has to be gathered. For assistance in performing these tasks, Utah legislators, having few staff services and possessing relatively little experience, are particularly dependent upon lobbyists. Thus, attitudes alone do not explain the nature of the Utah legislative system.

The Utah legislators' attitudes are perhaps traceable to the fact that two thirds of those legislators are Mormons (even though less than half the population of the state is Mormon). Utah is the only state in which a single religio-economic group controls a majority of the seats in the legislature. The dominance of the Mormon Church probably prejudices the attitude of legislators against other, "outside" groups. In addition, there is a stern moralism associated with the Utah legislature. This moralism seems to be reflected in the orientation booklet published by the legislature, a booklet which may be one source of the Utah legislator's hostile attitude toward lobbyists. The booklet addresses itself to the beginning legislator:

> Perhaps the most overwhelming experience for any new legislator is his first contact with the lobbyist—the person representing a special interest. Since each lobbyist is committed to advancing the cause of his own group, the legislator can expect to encounter considerable pressure to vote a narrowly seen "right way." There is nothing wrong with listening to the case presented by a lobbyist. He may provide valuable information. But the legislator should always remember that the lobbyist will volunteer only information which is helpful to his cause; that which is contrary must be learned elsewhere.[12]

In spite of these pressures against lobbyists, Utah still has a strong interest-group system.

Summary

This comparative analysis has probably raised more new questions than it has provided answers to existing questions. There seems to be little doubt that interest groups are very powerful in Oregon and very weak in Massachusetts. Very little would happen

[12] *The Utah Legislator's Orientation Manual* (1966), p. 6.

in Massachusetts if there were no lobbies, but, if lobbies disappeared in Oregon, the legislature would function in an entirely different fashion. On the other hand, it would be very difficult to say what the consequences would be in North Carolina and Utah if lobbies were to disappear, since the perceptions of legislators and lobbyists in those states, especially in North Carolina, are so incongruent. In Utah, furthermore, the high activity and moderately high impact of lobbyists is not matched by a favorable set of attitudes on the part of the legislators. Attitudinally, Utah is as similar to Massachusetts as it is to Oregon.

8 THE TECHNIQUES OF LOBBYING

The content of communication varies to some extent with its form. When a lobbyist is presenting prepared testimony at a formal committee hearing, the words he chooses will not be the same as when he is discussing legislation over a cup of coffee with a cooperative legislator. The legislator, in turn, will react differently in a public forum, such as a committee hearing, than he will in a personal conversation. There is, then, a distinction to be made between the public and the private communications of legislators and lobbyists.[1]

The Importance of Committee Hearings

Even though at least the more experienced lobbyists try to spend as much of their time as possible in informal, personal communication, a substantial portion of the interchange between legislators and lobbyists does take place in the relatively public forum of the committee hearing. The committee hearing is generally the most important source of information for legislators, and lobbyists tend to flock to the committee rooms as the focal point of their contact with legislators. Naturally, the importance of committees varies

[1] For a discussion of the distinction between public and private behavior, see Erving Goffman, *The Presentation of Self in Everyday Life* (Garden City. N.Y.: Doubleday and Co., 1959).

with the structure of the legislature. For example, while more than three fourths of the legislators in Massachusetts, North Carolina, and Oregon indicate that committee hearings are their single most important source of information, only 48 percent of the Utah legislators respond in this fashion. The relative unimportance of committee hearings as a source of information in Utah can be explained at least partially by the fact that in that state standing committees must act upon all bills referred to them within ten calendar days in the House and eight calendar days in the Senate (unless the committee has the permission of the respective chambers to take longer). Thus, legislative committees in Utah do not have the authority to kill legislation by failing to act upon it. In fact, most of the Utah committees keep bills less than the maximum time allotted to them.[2]

A somewhat analogous situation exists in Massachusetts. Because of the constitutional right of the people in that state to petition the legislature directly, and because of cultural support for this legal principle, the Massachusetts legislature is even busier than the Utah legislature. Any citizen in Massachusetts may submit any number of proposals on any subject for legislative consideration. Although it is true that these petitions must have the endorsement of the petitioner's representative or senator before being given serious consideration, legislators seldom refuse to grant endorsement.[3] Further, it is customary for all petitions to be given a public hearing before a legislative committee, and they must be reported out of the committee and sent to the floor. In other words, as in Utah, legislative committees in Massachusetts cannot pigeonhole legislation. In spite of this similarity between the two states, however, Massachusetts legislators are somewhat more inclined to look to committee hearings for information than are Utah legislators; but they are less

[2] Utah Legislative Council, Legislative Study Committee, *Final Report* (Salt Lake City, 1966), pp. 91–100. The Utah legislature as a whole is a relatively busy one, judging by the number of bills it considers per day. The legislature handles 17 bills per day, second only in this respect to the Massachusetts legislature. The busiest committees in the Senate and House in Utah are the State, Federal and Military Affairs Committees. In the House, in 1963, this committee considered 55 bills for about one week each; in the Senate, this committee considered 67 bills about four days each. These two busy committees devoted just about as much time to each bill as did some of the relatively inactive committees, such as the labor committees of the respective chambers.

[3] Barry M. Portnoy, ''The Legislative System in the Massachusetts House of Representatives'' (Senior Honors Thesis, Harvard University, 1967).

inclined to do so than are the legislators in either North Carolina or Oregon.

Even though there are variations in the institutional structure of committees, the fact remains that committee hearings by and large are a basic source of information for legislators. Indeed, they are *the* basic source of information in all states except Utah. The point is, of course, that the achieving of access to legislative decision makers is dictated to some extent by the structure of the information system. Rather than lurking around in lobbies looking mysterious, most lobbyists simply show up at a committee hearing and offer their testimony. This is not enough, as we shall see; but this is what lobbying means to most of its practitioners.

Interest Groups as Alternative Sources of Information

In addition to committee hearings, legislators tend to rely heavily on personal reading and research as sources of information. This is, of course, in contrast to national legislators, who enjoy the benefits of more adequate staffs. In fact, very few state legislators (except those in Massachusetts, who have the most extensive staff services) get any information at all from whatever meager staffs do exist. In some states, notably Utah, a legislative reference service provides considerable information. In general, however, the state legislator must depend for his information upon what he can learn by himself and what he can learn in the somewhat harried atmosphere of the committee hearing.

Where do interest groups fit into this picture? It is, perhaps, misleading to refer to Oregon and Utah as strong-lobby states unless we keep in mind that interest groups are strong in these states in comparison to their strengths in other states but not necessarily in comparison to other sources of information. Indeed, in Oregon, which we know as the state with the strongest lobbies, only 12 percent of the legislators indicate that interest groups are a primary source of information (except for their testimony in committee hearings).[4] Thus, we see that the role of interest groups in

---

[4] Even so, interest groups in Oregon are a more important source of information than is party leadership, a condition which does not hold true for any other state, including North Carolina with its tradition of weak party control.

the total distribution of information to legislators is not as important as we might think. This should not obscure the fact that
interest groups might still have considerable impact on legislative
decision making through activities centered in committee hearings.
It seems clear that communication unrelated to hearings is not very
important. However, it must be kept in mind that successful testimony before a committee requires considerable audience preparation, and that this preparation often takes the form of contacts with
committee members undertaken by the lobbyist before he appears at
the hearing. In fact, it is probably best to look upon the formal
hearing as a climax to a series of communications.

We must not ignore the fact that there are certain legislators who
look to interest groups as primary sources of information without
reference to hearings, although these legislators are a small minority. One way of examining this minority is to look at the number of
years of experience its members have had in the legislature. It
might be assumed that as legislators gain experience, they tend to
shun the formal committee and look for more confidential sources of
information. In the weak-lobby states, Massachusetts and North
Carolina, the more experienced legislators do, more often than the
beginning legislators, consider lobbyists to be a primary source of
information. If it will be recalled that these states are also those
with more heavily institutionalized folkways, it might seem reasonable to argue that beginning legislators of necessity rely on the
established and easily accessible methods of obtaining information,
whereas the more experienced legislators know the "right" lobbyist
to contact for their information. In the strong-lobby states, however, where rules of the game are more established with regard to
interaction with lobbyists than they are with regard to internal
procedure, the less experienced legislators are just as likely to rely
on lobbyists for information as are the more experienced ones. In
other words, interaction between legislators and lobbyists in these
states is so immediate that even freshmen legislators find it possible
—indeed, preferable—to shun committee hearings in favor of direct
communication with lobbyists.

Opportunities for lobbyists to establish personal communication
with legislators should be fairly good in Utah, since, as we have
seen, committee hearings are less important in that state than in
any other. However, in spite of the relative unimportance of committee hearings, Utah legislators do not look upon lobbyists as a
primary source of information. Rather, they prefer (if they do not

rely on the evidence of committee hearings) to gather their information by means of personal research. More Utah legislators prefer this method than do legislators in any other state, even though Utah legislators have no more adequate staff services than legislators in the other states. Given the hostile and suspicious attitude that Utah legislators have toward lobbyists, alternative sources of information to hearings, sources originating from within the legislature itself, have a greater chance of success. The Utah Legislative Council, for instance, attracts more attention than do comparable bodies in other states. Forty-five percent of Utah legislators list the legislative council as a primary information source, compared to about 12 percent of the legislators in the other states. Thus, Utah legislators seem almost anxious to avoid close reliance upon lobbyists. Indeed, the more legislative experience they acquire, the *less* likely they are to look to lobbyists as sources of information. This finding is somewhat puzzling in view of the fact that Utah legislators interact quite frequently with lobbyists and that their interaction increases with experience. However, if we recall our previous conclusions that the interaction between legislators and lobbyists in Utah seems a product less of a *desire* for interaction than of a *necessity* for interaction, these apparent discrepancies are not so bothersome. Although Utah legislators interact with lobbyists, they tend to look upon this interaction as unproductive of information. Thus, interaction, generally a very clear indicator of behavior, is not an efficient predictor of behavior for Utah legislators.

In the previous chapter, we examined the extent to which lobbyists try to concentrate their efforts upon the legislative leadership. We found that only in Massachusetts is this strategy attempted. If we examine the extent to which leaders and nonleaders rely upon lobbyists as primary sources of information, we find that their perceptions generally reflect the strategy of lobbyists in their respective states. The general pattern is that leaders do not rely upon lobbyists for information any more than do nonleaders. Leaders do tend to look upon the formal committee hearing as a source of information less than do nonleaders, but they do not allow lobbyists to take the place of committee hearings. In Massachusetts, although leaders interact somewhat more frequently with lobbyists than do nonleaders, this interaction does not produce greater utilization of lobbyists as information sources. In Massachusetts, as well as in North Carolina, there is no distinction between the extent to which leaders and nonleaders use lobbyists for information. In the strong-lobby states, however, nonleaders turn to lobbyists for information quite a bit more frequently than do leaders. This is especially evident in Oregon, where 26 percent of the nonleaders rely primarily on lobbyists for information, compared to 10 percent of the leaders. The figure for Oregon nonleaders represents the highest proportion of any legislative group relying upon lobbyists.

There is one case in which interaction and reliance upon lobbyists for information seem to run closely together. Republican legislators interact more closely with lobbyists and tend to rely upon them for information more extensively than do Democratic legislators. Since lobbyists are generally very careful about avoiding partisan statements or commitments, the closer relationship of lobbyists and Republicans is probably not related to overtly partisan issues. Rather, this close relationship might be linked to the fact that business lobbyists tend to dominate the representation of interests before the legislature, and legislators more often have business backgrounds than labor backgrounds. Since people with shared attitudes tend to interact more readily, it is easier for business lobbyists than for labor lobbyists to get to see Republican legislators. We noted that labor lobbyists engage in more typical "lobby" (that is to say, persuasive) activities than do business lobbyists. Now we find that Republican legislators (whom we presume to be more sympathetic to the business point of view) are easier targets. Thus, the business lobby can operate more silently than can the labor lobby.

Methods of Supplementing Testimony

Since the committee hearing is the major source of information for most legislators, it is natural for lobbyists to devote most of their time to formal testimony. However, if lobbyists rely solely upon testimony as a means of communication, without any supplementary efforts, the evidence suggests that the results will not be especially satisfying. If the lobbyist is to realize his maximum potential, he must look upon the presentation of testimony as a portion of a total communications process, a process which includes a variety of interpersonal and informal methods. The object of supplementary communication is to make the formal testimony credible. Lobbyists believe their testimony will be better received if the committee members know them personally and have been given some personal summary of the testimony. Table 8.1 indicates some of the methods used by lobbyists to improve their effectiveness at a hearing. The Table suggests that the techniques of lobbyists are governed to some extent by the characteristics of the system in which they operate. For instance, Utah lobbyists are exceptionally low in comparison to lobbyists in the other states with regard to their reliance on committee hearings. Indeed, Utah lobbyists are the only ones who consider other forms of communication more important than committee hearings. The rapidity with which hearings are conducted in Utah is probably contributory to the need lobbyists feel to exploit other possible methods of communication. These other methods are informal meetings with the committee, meetings perhaps conducted at a less hectic pace, and individual meetings by appointment with members of the committee.

Lobbyists in general place greater reliance upon prearranged meetings with legislators than upon chance meetings, but arranging a meeting seems to be less difficult in Utah than in the other states, especially Massachusetts. In Massachusetts, the most immediate alternative to personal communication with committee members—either in informal group meetings or by appointment—is the telephone. The necessity to interact with a large body of legislators deprives a Massachusetts lobbyist of the opportunity to "get around" as much as the lobbyists in other states.

Table 8.1 also indicates that lobbyists do not spend as much time as one might think at social gatherings. However, these data must be qualified by mention of the fact that lobbyists are not accustomed to thinking of social gatherings as a means of communication, but rather as a device to facilitate communication by other methods. It is also possible that lobbyists, whatever the interpretation they assign to the entertainment of legislators, cannot afford to entertain them very often. On the other hand, however, lobbyists also do not place much reliance upon written communications, which are, in contrast to entertainment, inexpensive devices. Whereas Milbrath found that Washington lobbyists prepare written summaries of their testimony to be submitted either before or after the oral presentation, very few state lobbyists take the trouble to do this.[5]

[5] Lester W. Milbrath, *The Washington Lobbyists* (Chicago: Rand McNally & Co., 1963), pp. 226–227.

TABLE 8.1

Methods of Communication with Legislators:
Percentages of Lobbyists Using Various Methods

	Massachusetts (N = 185)	North Carolina (N = 132)	Oregon (N = 193)	Utah (N = 134)
Committee hearings	40%	36%	48%	19%
Informal group meetings	22	15	12	29
Telephone calls	15	8	2	7
Chance meetings	4	8	10	8
Meetings by appointment	9	24	20	30
Social gatherings	4	2	2	0
Letters, reports	5	5	3	6

This divergence of technique is not necessarily due to laziness on the part of the state lobbyist. In view of the fact that there is relatively little direct, personal communication between Washington lobbyists and Washington legislators, the written summary may well be used there in lieu of follow-up tactics of a more personal nature, tactics which, as we have seen, are utilized by state lobbyists.

Other variations in the degree to which a method of communication is utilized are related to the predispositions, skills, and experience of the lobbyists themselves. One way of examining these variations is to look at lobbyists in terms of the length of time they have been practicing their profession. Beginning lobbyists, one might suspect, are apt to spend all of their time at committee hearings, because they have not yet learned of the other available approaches to legislators. However, this assumption is not borne out at all by the evidence. In every state except Massachusetts, the seasoned lobbyists actually spend more of their time at committee hearings than do the novices. It may be that the novice lobbyist, under the influence of the stereotype of lobbying, is trying to operate "behind closed doors," whereas the veteran has learned the value of well-prepared public testimony. Novices are also far more likely to try to contact legislators simply by bumping into them by chance. Veteran lobbyists will rarely, if ever, depend upon chance meetings. Rather, they are inclined to try to arrange a specific time during which they can present their point of view to a legislator who is prepared to listen and knows what to expect. Of course, setting up appointments with busy legislators is a time-consuming job, and it is perhaps easier just to rely upon chance.

As lobbyists themselves are anxious to point out, lobbying is, if done properly, a full-time job. If we examine lobbyists according to the number of hours per day they put in on the job, we find that those who spend the least amount of time at their jobs are more likely to rely upon chance meetings than the hard workers, who are more likely to rely upon meetings by appointment. The hard-working lobbyists are also more likely to spend their time writing summaries of their testimonies than are the "slackers." The telephone emerges as the most important supplementary instrument for those lobbyists who do not spend a great many hours on the job.

It might be suspected that the hard-working lobbyist would spend less of his time in committee hearings than would the slacker, but this is not the case. In all states except Utah, the hardest working lobbyists spend substantially more of their time in committee hearings than do the less active ones. In Utah, the hard-working lobbyists avoid committee hearings and devote their communication efforts to informal group meetings and meetings by appointment. As we have observed, the role of the hearing is relatively minor in Utah.

Perhaps the clearest patterns associated with the distributions of the lobbyists' time are those patterns related to the self-perceptions of lobbyists and the perceptions that others have of them with regard to their success. These factors operate independently of such variables as length of time lobbying and number of hours on the job, and suggest more clearly what lobbyists consider to be the most important targets for their efforts. Let us look first at the lobbyists considered by their colleagues and by legislators to be influential, as contrasted to those lobbyists considered to be without influence. In general, influential lobbyists do not rely upon committee hearings as much as do less influential ones. This pattern is especially conspicuous in Massachusetts and Utah, where institutional factors deflate the value of committee hearings. The alternative to hearings most clearly preferred by influential lobbyists is the meeting by appointment. In every state, those lobbyists considered to be powerful are substantially more likely to rely upon such meetings than are their less successful colleagues. The notion that successful lobbyists do not depend exclusively upon the committee hearing is corroborated if we look at lobbyists' estimations of the extent to which they have persuaded legislators to modify their positions. In every state, those lobbyists who score high on the persuasibility index are less inclined to rely on hearings than are those who score low. The differences are minimal in Utah, where neither the low nor high scorers place much faith in hearings. Lobbyists who perceive themselves as successful are far more likely to rely upon meetings by appointment than those lobbyists who do not consider themselves successful. This is especially striking in Massachusetts, where the fewest number of lobbyists rely upon meetings by appointment. Only 9 percent of all Massachusetts lobbyists use this technique, compared to about one fourth of all lobbyists in other states. Yet 32 percent of the Massachusetts lobbyists who score high on the persuasibility index rely upon this technique, compared to 1 percent of those who score low. In the other states the differences are not as striking, but the direction is the same.

Thus, the evidence suggests that lobbyists who devote themselves exclusively to the task of testifying before committees are misinterpreting the nature of their jobs. As one lobbyist expressed it:

> If you walk into a committee hearing and nobody knows who you are, your testimony is not likely to make much difference. If you have to spend a lot of time explaining who you are, who you represent, why you are here, and so forth, everybody gets bored. If they are not familiar with the organization you represent, they are likely to consider you as some sort of interloper. So what you have to do is to cultivate their friendship long in advance of the actual hearing. As soon as I know who will be on the committee, even before the first meeting is held, I make certain that they have at least met me. Since you frequently have to deal with freshmen who have never seen you or heard of you, this can be a pretty difficult job.

The task of developing a basis for interaction is facilitated to some extent by the absence of strong seniority rules in state legislatures. Regardless of their seniority, legislators tend to be assigned to committees whose subject matter relates to their occupational experience. As Jewell and Patterson point out, lawyers are assigned to the judiciary committee, insurance men to the insurance committee, and farmers to the agriculture committee.[6] This means that there is at least the possibility that the lobbyist and legislator have some basis for a relationship in addition to that growing from their exchange within the legislature. Even if they have no previous personal relationship, it is likely that the shared interests of these legislators and lobbyists will facilitate efficient communication.

However, one group of lobbyists stands to gain very little from the practice of assigning legislators to committees on the basis of occupational experience. Since very few state legislators have backgrounds in organized labor, labor lobbyists have little opportunity to interact with like-minded legislators. Labor committees will not be stacked in favor of labor lobbyists as business-oriented committees might be stacked in favor of business lobbyists, and, thus, the establishment of successful communications is more difficult for the labor lobbyist. Perhaps for this reason, we find that labor lobbyists are much less likely to rely upon hearings than are business lobbyists (except in Utah, where committee hearings do not assume the importance that they do in other states). Here again we find labor

---

[6] Malcolm E. Jewell and Samuel C. Patterson, *The Legislative Process in the United States* (New York: Random House, 1966), p. 228.

operating under somewhat of a handicap. The handicap is especially observable in Massachusetts, where labor lobbyists are substantially more likely to rely upon the telephone and written communications—although these are considered less desirable methods of communication—while business lobbyists find it easier to arrange meetings by appointment. Labor lobbyists frequently try to supplement their testimony by enlisting the support of friendly legislators; business lobbyists do not. Labor lobbyists also believe that their arguments will be given a more hospitable reception if they can arrange for an intermediary to do their lobbying for them, whereas business lobbyists are willing to face the committee alone. A common device among labor lobbyists is to arrange for union members to testify at hearings in place of the lobbyist himself. This is done in an effort to establish legitimacy and credibility. Such problems simply do not bother business lobbyists.

Of course, the way the labor lobbyists spend their time might not be the way they prefer to spend it. For example, although they use the telephone quite a bit, they may well wish that they could spend more time in methods of communication which they perceive to be more effective but are restrained from doing so because of the contingencies of the situation. Legislators might not want to take the time to spend with them in, for example, personal presentation of arguments. Milbrath found that lobbyists in Washington would like to spend more time in personal communication, but are unable to do so. The same problem bothers state labor lobbyists but not state business lobbyists, or, at least, not to the same extent.

The Perceived Effectiveness of Various Techniques

In order to get an idea which techniques of communication lobbyists believe to be most effective, we asked both legislators and lobbyists to evaluate a series of techniques for bringing home a point to a public official. Respondents were asked to rate each technique on a scale ranging from 0 (meaning absolutely ineffective) to 8 (indicating maximum effectiveness). From these responses, we calculated the mean effectiveness of each technique, as rated by each set of respondents (see Table 8.2). We grouped techniques—in a manner similar to that of Milbrath in his study of Washington lobbyists—into four general categories.[7]

The first category, which Milbrath calls *direct, personal communications*, consists of personal presentation of arguments, presentation of research results, and testimony at hearings. As our earlier findings would lead us to suspect, these direct techniques are perceived by both legislators and lobbyists to be most effective.

The second category, *communication through an intermediary*, consists of contacts between the legislator and his constituents or close friends arranged by the lobbyist. Milbrath includes within this category such indirect techniques as letter and telegram campaigns, public relations campaigns, and the publicizing of voting records. However, for our purposes it is more useful to consider communication through intermediaries as consisting only of direct contact by a third party, and to place the remainder of Milbrath's techniques under a separate heading, which we will call *indirect, impersonal communication*.

Milbrath's final category, which he calls *methods of keeping communication channels open*, does not in reality consist of techniques of actual influence. With this category, Milbrath is suggesting quite correctly that there are certain techniques which, while themselves not directly related to the exchange of influence, are still important in that they set the scene for more immediate interaction. Such techniques as entertainment, bribery, and campaign contributions are included in this category.

Personal Communication

As noted earlier, both legislators and lobbyists rate personal communication as the most effective lobbying technique. Table 8.2 indicates that among both groups of respondents, the three particular methods falling in this category outrank all other methods in their perceived effectiveness. Of these three methods, as we would expect, lobbyists rank personal presentation of arguments highest as a means of bringing home a point. There is practically no variation in lobbyists' evaluation of this technique among the four states considered here, and the Washington lobbyists interviewed by

[7] See Milbrath, pp. 392–393. Milbrath's responses are coded from 0 to 10. In order to make it possible to compare our data to Milbrath's, his data were recoded.

Milbrath also consider this their most effective technique. Lobbyists everywhere, in other words, consider personal presentation of arguments to be more effective than either the presentation of research results or testimony at hearings, even though they spend more of their time presenting testimony than they do in personal presentation of arguments. Here we find, therefore, that the most effective technique is one which lobbyists cannot engage in as much as they would like. The problem is the same in Washington as in the states, but, as Milbrath's research suggests, it is more acute in Washington.

Comparison of the responses of legislators and lobbyists in this or any other category is made difficult by the tendency of lobbyists to offer high evaluations for all techniques. Lobbyists generally consider most of their techniques to be more effective than legislators consider them to be. In comparing the raw scores of the two groups, therefore, the constant difference in means might tend to obscure variations in responses. To correct this, we can recompute the deviations of these ratings from the mean for all techniques (see Table 8.3). This computation allows us to compare perceptions of various techniques without being over-influenced by the bias of lobbyists, who tend to rate techniques higher than do legislators. We now notice that lobbyists consider the personal presentation of arguments to be more effective than do legislators (except in Oregon), whereas legislators consider the presentation of research results and the testimony of the lobbyist at hearings to be more effective than do lobbyists. As one would expect, both legislators and lobbyists in Utah consider testimony at hearings to be less effective than do the comparable respondents in other states. But, in general, lobbyists consider personal presentation of arguments to be the most effective technique of communication; legislators consider the presentation of research results to be the most effective technique. Here again we encounter the familiar discrepancy between the role orientations of legislators and lobbyists. We noted in previous chapters that lobbyists tend to view their communication with legislators as persuasive, but that legislators like to think of their communication with lobbyists as informational. From this, we would naturally expect legislators to assign a higher value to a technique of communication—such as the presentation of research results—which appears to be purely informational.

Also to be noted is the fact that both legislators and lobbyists consider testimony at hearings to be the least effective direct method

TABLE 8.2
Ratings of Methods of Communication

	Massachusetts		North Carolina		Oregon		Utah	
	Legis-lators	Lobby-ists	Legis-lators	Lobby-ists	Legis-lators	Lobby-ists	Legis-lators	Lobby-ists
DIRECT, PERSONAL COMMUNICATION								
Personal presentation of arguments	5.8*	6.6	4.7	6.7	6.7	6.9	5.3	6.4
Presenting research results	6.0	5.8	5.4	5.4	6.8	6.0	6.3	5.5
Testifying at hearings	5.2	5.6	4.8	5.3	6.1	5.7	5.1	5.0
COMMUNICATION THROUGH AN INTERMEDIARY								
Contact by constituent	2.5	3.2	3.0	5.4	2.7	4.3	3.6	5.0
Contact by friend	2.0	2.5	3.0	4.2	2.4	3.7	3.4	4.0
Contact by other lobbyists	2.4	4.3	2.5	4.2	3.2	4.5	3.0	4.8
INDIRECT, IMPERSONAL COMMUNICATION								
Letter writing campaign	2.0	3.4	1.7	4.0	1.6	4.0	2.8	4.0
Publication of voting records	2.0	2.2	1.3	1.4	1.5	2.0	2.0	2.4
Public relations campaign	3.5	3.7	3.5	4.6	3.5	4.0	4.1	4.6
KEEPING CHANNELS OPEN								
Entertaining legislators	1.0	1.3	2.0	2.5	1.7	2.2	2.8	3.0
Giving a party	1.0	1.0	2.0	1.8	1.4	1.6	2.4	2.3
Campaign contributions	1.0	2.0	1.6	2.4	1.5	2.5	2.1	3.3
Withholding campaign contributions	.3	.1	.3	.4	.1	.1	1.0	1.0
Bribery	.2	.1	.1	1.2	.03	.2	.2	.3
MEAN FOR ALL TECHNIQUES	2.5	3.0	2.6	3.5	2.8	3.5	3.2	3.7

* Ratings of effectiveness on a scale from 0 (ineffective) to 8 (effective).

TABLE 8.3

Ratings of Methods of Communication, Adjusted as Deviation from Mean*

	Massachusetts		North Carolina		Oregon		Utah	
	Legis-lators	Lobby-ists	Legis-lators	Lobby-ists	Legis-lators	Lobby-ists	Legis-lators	Lobby-ists
DIRECT, PERSONAL COMMUNICATION								
Personal presentation of arguments	3.3	3.6	2.1	3.2	3.9	3.4	2.1	2.7
Presenting research results	3.5	2.8	2.8	1.9	4.0	2.5	3.1	1.8
Testifying at hearings	2.7	2.6	2.2	1.8	3.3	2.2	1.9	1.3
COMMUNICATION THROUGH AN INTERMEDIARY								
Contact by constituent	0	.2	.4	1.9	−.1	.8	.4	1.3
Contact by friend	−.5	−.5	.4	.7	−.3	.2	.2	.3
Contact by other lobbyists	−.1	1.3	−.1	.7	.4	1.0	−.2	1.1
INDIRECT, IMPERSONAL COMMUNICATION								
Letter writing campaign	−.5	.4	−.9	.5	−1.2	.5	−.4	.3
Publication of voting records	−.5	−1.2	−1.3	−2.1	−1.3	−1.5	−1.2	−1.3
Public relations campaign	1.5	.7	.9	1.1	.7	.5	.9	.9
KEEPING CHANNELS OPEN								
Entertaining legislators	−1.5	−1.7	−.6	−1.0	−1.1	−1.3	−.4	−.7
Giving a party	−1.5	−2.0	−.6	−1.7	−1.4	−1.9	−.8	−1.4
Campaign contributions	−1.5	−1.0	−1.0	−1.0	−1.3	−1.0	−1.1	−.4
Withholding campaign contributions	−2.2	−2.9	−2.3	−3.1	−2.7	−3.4	−2.2	−2.7
Bribery	−2.3	−2.9	−2.5	−3.3	−2.8	−4.3	−3.0	−3.4

* The mean in each state for all methods of communication, as rated by legislators and lobbyists.

178

of communication. This finding underscores the comments of the previous section, where it was suggested that testimony at hearings must be supplemented with other forms of communication. At the same time, it should not be overlooked that lobbyists consider the "personal touch" to be more important than legislators do in the achieving of a satisfactory result. The general consensus about the effectiveness of direct communication apparently operates to reduce the significance of the interstate variables which have dominated our findings to this point.

State variations do not affect perceptions of the importance of direct communication, but we are curious as to the extent to which the process of socialization associated with the careers of legislators and lobbyists operates to change perceptions of the best way to go about the job of lobbying. Three measures will help us understand the changing orientations of legislators and lobbyists: length of time on the job, extent of interaction, and degree of persuasibility. In Table 8.4, a positive sign indicates that perceptions of effectiveness increase with a given variable; a negative sign indicates a decrease in perception of effectiveness; and a zero indicates no change with the independent variable. The fact that there is no change with the independent variable should not be taken to mean that the particular technique is not effective. Indeed, just the reverse might be true.

We note first that in most cases the tendency is for perception of effectiveness to increase with experience. Among legislators, there are five instances of increasing perception of effectiveness, four cases of no change in perception, and three cases of decreasing perception of effectiveness. Among lobbyists, there are six cases of increasing perception of effectiveness, two cases of no change, and four cases of decreasing perception. In general, therefore, the longer one has been engaged in the occupation of either legislating or lobbying, the more likely he is to believe that direct, personal communication is most effective. Massachusetts, however, is an exception. In none of the three examples of direct communication do perceptions of effectiveness increase in Massachusetts. Indeed, among lobbyists, there is a uniform tendency for a decrease to occur, casting light once again upon the discouraged attitude of the Massachusetts lobbyist. Lobbyists in Massachusetts stand in clear contrast to lobbyists in Oregon, who uniformly display an increase in confidence in their techniques as they acquire more experience.

The relationship between interaction and evaluations of the effec-

TABLE 8.4

Changes in Evaluation of Methods of Direct, Personal Communication with Length of Time in the Occupation, Interaction, and Persuasibility

	Massachusetts		North Carolina		Oregon		Utah	
	Legis-lators	Lobby-ists	Legis-lators	Lobby-ists	Legis-lators	Lobby-ists	Legis-lators	Lobby-ists
LENGTH OF TIME IN THE OCCUPATION								
Personal presentation of arguments	0	−	+	+	0	+	+	+
Presenting research results	−	−	0	−	+	+	0	0
Testifying at hearings	−	−	+	0	+	+	−	+
INTERACTION								
Personal presentation of arguments	+	0	+	−	+	0	+	0
Presenting research results	+	−	+	0	+	−	−	−
Testifying at hearings	0	−	0	0	0	0	−	−
PERSUASIBILITY								
Personal presentation of arguments	0	+	0	+	−	+	0	+
Presenting research results	−	0	0	+	0	−	0	0
Testifying at hearings	0	0	0	+	0	+	−	−

tiveness of direct personal communication is somewhat different from the relationship between those evaluations and experience. This is true even though interaction and experience are related. For legislators, even in Massachusetts, the general pattern is for effectiveness of direct techniques to increase with increasing interaction. Only in Utah is there a decrease in perception of effectiveness as interaction increases. This occurs in the cases of both presentation of research results and testimony at hearings. We noted earlier that the interaction rate of Utah legislators is not especially helpful in predicting their reaction to lobbyists, since interaction is not as clearly related to favorable attitude in Utah as it is in other states. The interaction of Utah legislators and lobbyists seems almost forced. Here, we have further evidence to support this conclusion.

Among lobbyists, increasing interaction produces no increase in perceptions of the effectiveness of direct lobbying techniques. In half the sample, increased interaction produces decreased perceptions of effectiveness; in the other half, it produces no change whatever. It appears, therefore, that, with regard to the perceived effectiveness of direct lobbying, interaction has a positive effect upon legislators but a negative effect upon lobbyists. In view of the generally optimistic perceptions of lobbyists, this finding is difficult to interpret. We know that interaction and legislators' persuasibility are related; therefore, it is reasonable that those legislators with the most frequent interaction perceive the methods of communication under discussion here as more effective than do those legislators with the least interaction. Ironically, however, the more that lobbyists interact with legislators, the less control they believe themselves to have over the outcome of legislative decision making. It seems, therefore, that interaction with legislators induces a fatalistic attitude among lobbyists that is not necessarily shared by legislators.

On the other hand, the pattern is reversed when we plot persuasibility against perceptions of effectiveness. Here, the tendency is for lobbyists who believe themselves able to change legislators' minds to increase their perception of the effectiveness of direct techniques. Yet, among legislators, persuasibility is, in most cases, unrelated to the perceived effectiveness of a given technique. Perhaps this is the key to the lobbyist's dilemma. The real payoff in the lobbying process is, of course, the inducing of legislators to adopt the lobbyist's point of view. While lobbyists believe they can induce such changes by manipulation of the manner of presentation of their case, the truth of the matter seems to be that the effectiveness of a lobbyist is not as clearly related to the techniques he employs as he thinks. In only one case (Oregon legislators evaluating personal presentation of arguments) is there any relationship of a positive nature between the extent to which a legislator is persuaded by a lobbyist and the legislator's evaluation of the techniques of the lobbyist. On the other hand, there are relatively few examples of techniques decreasing in perceived effectiveness as persuasibility of legislators increases, which suggests again that persuasibility and perception of techniques are not related. The absence of a relationship between persuasibility and perceptions of techniques may be due, in part, to the fact that the techniques under consideration here are generally perceived to be the most effective techniques available to the lobbyist. These techniques, therefore, might not be subject to as much variation as some of the less effective techniques. Yet personal presentation of arguments, which is considered by lobbyists to be their most effective technique, shows the greatest variation with the three independent variables. Let us suggest, therefore, that in the way a technique is perceived there is more at stake for lobbyists than for legislators. Thus, while for legislators there is no relationship between the independent variable and perception of effectiveness of techniques in fifteen of the cases displayed on the table, a similar lack of relationship is true for lobbyists in only eleven cases. Given the necessity for a pleasing self-image on the parts of lobbyists (as, indeed, on the part of anyone engaged in any occupation), it would be important for them to believe that their skills contribute more to the outcome of legislative deliberations than may actually be the case.

However, one should not conclude that certain techniques are of no value merely because they apparently produce little or no change in the persuasibility of legislators. It must also be kept in mind that there are few cases in which the use of these techniques and persuasibility are *negatively* related. In other words, proper use of such techniques can *maximize* the influence of lobbyists even though the source of this influence is to be found not in the efforts of the lobbyist, but in the social position of the lobbyist and his image in the minds of legislators. Evaluations of techniques vary with the styles of lobbyists. Style, as we noted in our comparison of business and labor lobbyists, varies with the type of organization being represented. As Table 8.5 indicates, business lobbyists give a substantially higher rating to direct, personal communication than do

TABLE 8.5

Evaluations of Methods of Direct Personal Communication by Business Lobbyists and Labor Lobbyists* (as Deviation from Mean**)

| | Massachusetts | | Oregon | | Utah | |
	Business (N = 50)	Labor (N = 13)	Business (N = 98)	Labor (N = 33)	Business (N = 54)	Labor (N = 14)
Personal presentation of arguments	3.5	1.6	3.3	2.8	3.3	1.5
Presenting research results	2.3	1.0	2.3	1.5	2.1	.8
Testifying at hearings	2.6	.0	1.9	.3	1.2	.8

* North Carolina excluded because of lack of labor lobbyists.

** The mean in each state for all methods of communication, as rated by business lobbyists and labor lobbyists.

labor lobbyists. We find here that these differences in style produce concomitant differences in evaluations of techniques. Labor lobbyists, being unable to rely upon direct communication exclusively, find it necessary to utilize supplementary techniques; they are therefore inclined to devaluate the effectiveness of the personal exchange. Business lobbyists, whose direct access to legislators is more easily achieved, attribute a greater effectiveness to direct communication. The labor lobbyist's inability to achieve direct communication necessitates his reliance upon the second category of communications, the use of intermediaries.

The Use of Intermediaries

Lobbyists consider the intervention of third parties as a less efficient mechanism of influence than direct communication. If we examine the responses of lobbyists and legislators with regard to intervention by constituents, friends, and other organizations, we find that all three types of intermediate communication fall well below the direct approach in perceived effectiveness. However, the two groups of respondents differ substantially in their perception of which of the three classes of intermediaries is more or less preferable. Milbrath found that Washington lobbyists prefer that constituents, rather than close personal friends of the legislator, play the role of intermediary.[8] The same finding is characteristic of the attitudes of state lobbyists. In every state except Utah, lobbyists believe that a constituent can do a better job with a legislator than can a friend. Among legislators, however, as Milbrath also found to be true in Washington, constituents are thought no more (or less) effective than friends.

But the greatest discrepancy between perceptions of legislators and lobbyists with regard to the use of intermediaries occurs in the case of the use by the lobbyist of other lobbyists. Perhaps because they see more of other lobbyists than they do of either constituents or close friends of legislators, lobbyists are inclined to consider their colleagues as valuable agents of persuasion; legislators, however, are clearly not so inclined. Again, the probable explanation for the higher rating on the part of the lobbyist is the fact that other lobbyists are on the scene and available. This is especially important

---

[8] Milbrath, p. 240.

if time is short. There may well be no opportunity to arrange for constituent contact and the lobbyist may be unaware of who the legislator's friends are. Thus, in all four states, legislators place the intervention by another lobbyist either close to or beneath the mean effectiveness of all techniques, whereas lobbyists place it higher than the mean.

This discrepancy in the evaluations of the two groups on this particular technique deserves comment, as it relates to one of the standard components of the methodology of lobbying. The formation of coalitions has been thought to be one of the most effective weapons in the arsenal of interest groups; for some reason, it has been assumed that the mustering of support from more than one source is likely to have a positive result. Perhaps this assumption is derived from the democratic notion that there is a relationship between numbers and merit. In any case, as we have seen, legislators are not especially impressed with the intervention of a third party, even if it is a constituent. Thus, legislators are less inclined than lobbyists to consider the use of intermediaries effective. However, in spite of the tendency of lobbyists to place more reliance upon these techniques than they apparently merit, it should not be forgotten that lobbyists correctly rate these techniques as less effective than direct communication. Furthermore, as lobbyists acquire experience, they tend to place less reliance upon the use of intermediaries. Only in Massachusetts, where relations between legislators and lobbyists are hostile and suspicious, is there a positive relationship between experience and the perceived effectiveness of intermediaries. Also only in Massachusetts is there a positive relationship between legislators' evaluations of indirect communication and persuasibility.

In all four states, however, there is a positive relationship between interaction and the extent to which both legislators and lobbyists consider intermediaries to be an effective mode of communication. Since we also found a positive relationship between interaction and the perceived effectiveness of direct communication, it is probably the case that interaction, which induces legislators to become sympathetic with the responsibilities and problems of lobbyists, also induces legislators to accept any method of communication as legitimate.

The use of intermediaries is also a device relied upon when direct channels of access are blocked. For this reason, labor lobbyists are inclined to evaluate the use of intermediaries as more effective than are business lobbyists. Labor lobbyists are substantially more impressed with the use of all classes of intermediaries, but are especially anxious to work with other lobbyists. They are not as anxious to approach close friends of legislators as are business lobbyists, perhaps because they believe that the close friend of the legislator will not be any more amenable to their arguments than is the legislator himself.

The use by labor lobbyists of other lobbyists to influence legislators—and the relatively high rating they give this technique—raises the question of the nature of the relationships that exist among lobbyists, a point we discussed in earlier chapters. In general, the utilization of their colleagues by labor lobbyists requires a very high level of interaction among lobbyists with potentially conflicting interests. There is little advantage in one labor lobbyist asking another labor lobbyist to contact a legislator unless the difficulty in the relationship between the first lobbyist and the legislator is simply something idiosyncratic. For example, it occasionally occurs that a lobbyist's personality is so abrasive that he cannot interact with a given legislator and will, therefore, arrange for another lobbyist, of similar ideological persuasion, to do the job for him. However, labor lobbyists usually try to find business lobbyists who will help them out. If a business lobbyist and a labor lobbyist can cooperate, the labor lobbyist's chances for gaining access to the legislator are improved. Naturally, such a collaboration can occur only when business and labor are not in direct conflict over the issue involved. Such a situation occurs more frequently than might be thought. There is some collaboration between potentially competing lobbyists in all states. Labor lobbyists in Oregon, however, consider the use of colleagues as more effective than do labor lobbyists in any other state, probably because there is a more clearly established code of cooperation among Oregon lobbyists. The general rule is that any lobbyist will help a colleague if his own interest is not involved. In other words, a labor lobbyist can request and receive the help of a business lobbyist with a legislative problem if the business lobbyist considers his organization to have no direct interest in the outcome of the problem. However, the business lobbyist will withdraw his help if he discovers that a third lobbyist, whatever his organization, has a direct interest in the problem. Therefore, collaboration between labor and business lobbyists occurs primarily when the issue involved is simply one of stimulating the legislature to act. The rule, as stated by a lobbyist, is "You can't try to beat another lobbyist unless you have some real reason for doing so."

As an example of the use of other lobbyists as intermediaries, consider the following account. In 1965, in Oregon, an amendment to the constitution prohibiting public employees from serving in the legislature was being considered. Labor, believing that legislators who had been public employees were generally more sympathetic to its cause than legislators with business or professional backgrounds, opposed the amendment but discovered that eight of the members of the Constitutional Revision Committee were prepared to support it. The labor lobbyists tried to cooperate with education lobbyists in an attempt to influence committee members, but found that legislators identified the two organizations as representing similar interests and were not inclined to change their minds. Finally, the labor lobbyists went to representatives of the private power lobby, the trucking lobby, and the insurance lobby. Each of these business lobbyists, deciding that their organizations did not oppose the position of labor and discovering that no other lobbyist really cared one way or the other, agreed to help. The cooperation of the business lobbyists was due to their acceptance of the rules of the game in Oregon, rather than to any expectation of an exchange of favors. Even though labor lobbyists in Oregon are relatively well received in comparison with labor lobbyists in other states, there are still few legislators to whom they have clear and easy access. They are, therefore, of little use to business lobbyists who might be seeking intermediaries. In general, thus, most of the intervention on the part of lobbyists is performed by business lobbyists in support of their less accepted colleagues.

In some states, however, labor lobbyists seldom approach a business lobbyist even when business and labor interests do not conflict. Very little collaboration occurs, for example, in Massachusetts. In Massachusetts, most of the interaction among lobbyists is between those who have similar values. For example, labor lobbyists are more likely to request help from civil rights or education lobbyists than they are from business lobbyists. Since business dominates the legislature in Massachusetts to a lesser extent than in other states, there is less necessity on the part of nonbusiness lobbyists to seek secondhand legitimacy from business lobbyists.

Another unique feature of the Massachusetts system is the low evaluation by lobbyists of the use of constituents and friends as agents of influence. Whereas Massachusetts lobbyists consider other lobbyists as useful allies (although this collaboration is limited to those with similar ideological positions), they do not consider either constituents or friends as useful as do lobbyists of other states. It is curious that, in a state with as competitive a party system as Massachusetts, constituents are considered to be relatively ineffective. In general, it seems that Massachusetts lobbyists consider legislators to be relatively impervious to influence from outside the legislature itself. Exactly why they give such a relatively high ranking to the intervention of other lobbyists is difficult to understand, in view of the fact that they also assume that no lobbyists are very successful in pleading any cause before the legislature. Perhaps the most likely explanation is that the Massachusetts lobbyist, in reality, does not have the opportunity to call upon his colleagues in the profession as much as he would like to. Thus, evaluations of collaboration are based less upon experience than upon supposition.

Indirect, Impersonal Communication

The third category consists of techniques which do not involve a direct confrontation between the legislator and the lobbyist or any of the lobbyist's intermediaries. With these techniques the lobbyist attempts to stimulate communications to the legislator from a larger public. The lobbyist's assumption here is that the conflict must be enlarged beyond the confines of the legislative arena. The lobbyist is attempting to demonstrate to the legislator that his position is shared by a broader segment of the population, although in most cases this "broader" segment of the population consists mainly of the members of the interest group. The three methods of stimulating a broader interest in legislation—mass letter and telegram campaigns, publication of voting records, and the institution of public relations efforts—are all directed primarily toward the members of the interest group and are only incidentally concerned with nonmembers. Of these three methods, public relations campaigns are considered to be the most effective by both legislators and lobbyists. The publication of voting records is seen to be the least effective of these techniques, with the stimulation of letter and telegram campaigns falling between the two extremes. There is substantial consensus on this ranking of methods among the state legislators and lobbyists of our sample, a consensus similar to that reported by Milbrath in his study of lobbying in Washington.

The most apparent reason for the ineffectiveness of the publication of voting records is that it is perceived as a threat. Lobbyists resort to this technique when they wish to demonstrate to a legislator that his position is known to a segment of the population which has the power to defeat him at the polls. Since legislators rarely believe such a threat can be made real, they are not inclined to take it very seriously. Lobbyists, for their part, have the impression that the members of their organization actually pay little attention to published voting records, and, therefore, lobbyists are inclined to consider such publications a waste of time. However, examining the scores of both legislators and lobbyists as they deviate from their respective means, we note that legislators are inclined to give the publication of voting records a higher score than are lobbyists. Thus, even though neither group considers the technique to be of much value in comparison to, for example, direct approaches by lobbyists, the legislators apparently retain some residual fear that perhaps under certain circumstances the publication of voting records might be damaging.

A similar pattern appears with regard to public relations campaigns, which both parties rate relatively highly. Although the difference between the evaluations of legislators and the evaluations of lobbyists is slight, the overall tendency is for legislators to attribute slightly more importance to public relations than lobbyists. On the other hand, lobbyists consider the stimulation of letter and telegram campaigns as somewhat more effective than do legislators.

In Washington, the evidence is that in most cases letter and telegram campaigns, public relations campaigns, and publication of voting results are poorly timed and of minimum impact.[9] Much the same is true of the states, but, in the states, there are further obstacles in the way of indirect communication methods. For instance, very few state-oriented interest groups have the money or the membership to enable them to utilize extensive public campaigns. Furthermore, since direct access to legislators is more easily achieved in the states, a state lobbyist has less to gain by resorting to techniques which are clumsy and to some extent beyond his control. For example, although lobbyists may consider it advantageous to let the legislator know he is being observed by a broader public, they worry about the amateur nature of letter and telegram campaigns. Public relations campaigns, however, are not so likely to

[9] See, for example, Raymond A. Bauer, Ithiel de Sola Pool, and Lewis Anthony Dexter, *American Business and Public Policy* (New York: Atherton Press, 1963), pp. 415–421.

be placed in the hands of amateurs, since they are usually conducted with the help of professional advertising firms.

Given the amount of risk involved in indirect, impersonal methods of communication, it is not surprising that perceptions of their
effectiveness generally decline with length of time on the job, interaction, and persuasibility. There is a clear exception to this rule,
however. In Massachusetts, both legislators and lobbyists gain a
higher evaluation of these techniques as they acquire experience,
increase the intensity of interaction, or (for legislators) become
more receptive to the activities of lobbyists. We have seen that
direct lobbying is practiced less in Massachusetts than in any other
state. Lobbying in Massachusetts is substantially more impersonal
than it is in other states. The relatively high estimate of the effectiveness of impersonal techniques is, perhaps, another example of
lobbyists rationalizing about the value of a technique which is
forced upon them by the circumstances of the environment. Similarly, it may be that legislators in Massachusetts also tend to assign
a relatively high value to these techniques simply because they are
more often exposed to them than are legislators in other states.

The extent to which a particular tactic is used is also related to
the nature of the interest group. Obviously, an organization with a
small membership is not as likely as an organization with a large
membership (such as a labor or education group) to rely upon
letter and telegram campaigns or upon publication of voting records. Still, there is no reason why smaller organizations, if they
have the money, could not rely upon public relations campaigns,
since these are generally oriented toward the achievement in the
long run of a climate of opinion favorable to the influence of the
group and are not dependent upon the immediate response of a
limited membership.

Establishing a Framework for Communications

We consider now a variety of techniques which may be used to
establish a framework within which communication may take place.
These techniques are not, in themselves, to be regarded as devices
for the communication of influence or information from lobbyist to
legislator. Milbrath refers to such techniques as ''keeping communication channels open.'' In spite of the mythology about lobbying,
mythology which suggests that lobbyists throw wild parties, provide

numerous exotic entertainments, and dispense money with great abandon, these kinds of techniques are regarded by most respondents as being the least effective of all techniques available. Of course, a survey may not be the best way to ascertain the truth about the use of methods of keeping communication channels open. One of these methods, for example, is bribery, and we would hardly expect lobbyists or legislators to admit having offered or accepted bribes even if they are sure that the interview is totally anonymous. Indeed, the responses of the Massachusetts interviewees contrast sharply with revelations of the Massachusetts Crime Commission which suggest that corruption is a way of life in Massachusetts.[10] Nevertheless, it is highly probable that even in Massachusetts bribery and other forms of corruption are not characteristic of the entire population of legislators and lobbyists. Our data indicate *less* bribery in Massachusetts than the other states.[11]

Though all methods of keeping communication channels open are relatively ineffective, some, of course, are considered less ineffective than others. For example, both legislators and lobbyists in all states agree that entertainment and the contribution of money to campaigns are somewhat more effective than other techniques. Our data suggest that campaign contributions do stimulate legislators toward interaction, and this provides some support for the perceptions of legislators and lobbyists. Threatening not to contribute money is perceived to be a very ineffective technique for the same reason that publicizing voting records is given a low rating. Both are connotative of force and, thus, are not helpful in establishing a satisfactory basis for interaction.

Given the generally unsavory aspect of many of the techniques reported here, it is instructive to note that legislators give all these devices, with the exception of campaign contributions, a higher rating than do lobbyists. This is true even of bribery. Whereas both

[10] For an evaluation of the report of the Massachusetts Crime Commission, see James Q. Wilson, ''Corruption: The Shame of the States,'' *The Public Interest*, 2 (Winter 1966), 28–38.

[11] The following percentages of respondents indicate they have knowledge of bribery:

	Massachusetts	North Carolina	Oregon	Utah
Legislators	5%	10%	10%	14%
Lobbyists	7	15	9	12

The responses of legislators and lobbyists in Massachusetts may suggest either that there actually is less bribery in that state or that there was more evasion of our question. Our data alone cannot resolve this issue.

groups rank bribery as the least effective method, the overall legislative score deviates less from the mean than does the overall lobbyist score. Significantly, the least deviation from the mean occurs among Massachusetts respondents, both legislators and lobbyists. Perhaps the popular image of Massachusetts politics is reflected to some extent in the legislators' and lobbyists' evaluations of lobbying techniques. It should also be noticed that only in Massachusetts does perception of the effectiveness of techniques of this kind tend to increase instead of decrease with experience, interaction, and persuasibility.

Despite the low ranking given to entertainment, most lobbyists do as much entertaining as they can. There is a useful contrast to be made here between the state lobbying process and the Washington lobbying process. State lobbyists give entertainment and parties higher scores than Milbrath reports for Washington lobbyists. Milbrath notes that parties are so numerous in Washington that an invitation "becomes a punishment instead of a reward. The decision maker, who is required by his position and role to attend a large number of functions, treasures most highly the freedom to spend an evening at home with his family.'"[12] Such a situation is not characteristic of state legislators, who frequently are anxious to burn the candle at both ends. Since legislative sessions do not last very long, and since the social life in state capitals is considerably less developed than social life in Washington, state legislative sessions occasionally acquire the atmosphere of a long and extravagant house party. In Massachusetts, however, where sessions are virtually interminable, the situation is altogether different. There, entertainment is not ranked as highly as it is in other states. But, whatever the relative amount of entertaining done by the lobbyists of a particular state, it should be remembered that entertainment is a minor part of the *total* lobbying process, although it is a major part of that portion of the process concerned with establishing and maintaining communication channels.

A fundamental rule of the game with respect to entertainment is that entertainment should involve no discussion of business. If business is discussed, the point of entertainment is lost. As one lobbyist phrases it:

> The thing you don't do in circuit passing [lobbyist slang for running the gamut of bars and restaurants] is that you don't bother legislators about bills unless they want to talk about them.

[12] Milbrath, p. 271.

They want to relax, and, frankly, so do I. You are merely putting the legislator in the position of being more free with you the next day.

Another lobbyist makes the point quite explicitly:

We don't talk issues unless the legislator brings them up. The basic purpose is to get the legislator to call you by your first name. So much lobbying has to be done in a short span of time. You've got 30 seconds to talk to the guy and I don't want to spend any of this time introducing myself and telling him whom I represent.

Thus, it is quite clear that the object of entertainment is the facilitation of communication rather than the actual exchange of information.

The form of entertainment varies somewhat from state to state. In Utah, entertainment is typically a lunch-time affair of a rather austere nature. In Oregon, due to the heavily organized nature of the lobbying profession, entertainment frequently takes the form of formal affairs given by the entire corps of lobbyists for interested legislators. Included in these functions are an annual skit show, in which lobbyists lampoon legislators in the manner of the Washington press corps, and an annual beer party and softball game (which is, needless to say, always won by the legislators). The fact that Oregon lobbyists are able to provide such entertainment indicates the extent to which they are accepted as a legitimate part of the legislative process. In North Carolina, the most conspicuous example of large-scale entertaining is the custom of the Motor Carriers Association to provide a permanent buffet bar at one of the leading hotels in Raleigh. The bar is open to legislators throughout the legislative session, with free food and drink readily available. Many legislators take advantage of this largess.

In Massachusetts, lobbyists do not entertain as much as in other states and do not rank entertainment as highly. There is an interesting twist to the function of entertainment in Massachusettts. In that state, entertainment is used as a political tactic by legislators as well as lobbyists. Many Massachusetts lobbyists complain that they are required to purchase expensive tickets to testimonial dinners given by the friends of legislators and designed to raise money for legislators' campaigns. One lobbyist refers to this sort of pressure upon their resources as "operation clamp." In no other state has this technique of raising money from lobbyists been developed, although it has been going on in Washington for quite some time. Indeed, of all the states, the situation in Massachusetts seems to approximate most closely the situation in Washington.

Are Lobbyists Necessary?

The scant relationship between the persuasibility of legislators and their perceptions of the effectiveness of various techniques brings to mind a comment by Wahlke: ". . . reasons [given by legislators to explain an interest group's influence] connected with a group's claim to be represented or with its general political power appear, in almost every case, to be more significant than reasons associated with its lobbying activities in the legislative arena itself."[13] Wahlke, in suggesting that lobbying techniques alone do not account for a group's influence, leads one to wonder whether the various skills which lobbyists seek to develop are worth the effort. As a test of Wahlke's idea, we can examine the reasons that legislators and lobbyists give for their evaluations of the power of various groups. The word "power" in this case is freighted with ambiguities and perhaps should not be taken as a reliable measure of a group's actual achievement. For instance, educational associations are most frequently mentioned as powerful by Utah legislators and lobbyists, yet we have seen that Utah treats education with particular vengeance and that the activities of the Utah Education Association seem only to exacerbate an already hostile attitude. By the same token, religious groups receive practically no mention in heavily Mormon Utah (similarly, the Roman Catholic Church receives scant mention in Massachusetts), causing one to speculate that perhaps the most effective pressures upon the legislature are those that go unnoticed because they are so pervasive.

Along these lines, it is generally true, as it was in the case of perceptions of pressure, that perceptions of influence seem to be at least partially related to the general attitude that legislators have toward a given group. Thus, for example, the insurance industry in Massachusetts is perceived as powerful by 43 percent of the Republicans in the legislature of that state, as compared to 65 percent of the Democrats. However, more Republicans than Democrats in Mas-

---

[13] John C. Wahlke, Heinz Eulau, William Buchanan, and LeRoy C. Ferguson, *The Legislative System* (New York: John Wiley, 1962), p. 334.

sachusetts perceive labor unions as powerful. Similar patterns emerge in other states. Evaluations of power, then, are clearly related to the extent to which the legislator agrees with the group.

Given the fact that these rankings of powerful associations are somewhat suspect, we can, nevertheless, make some judgment as to the reasons for perceived power, especially as these reasons relate to the efforts of lobbyists. The following discussion considers groups which both legislators and lobbyists consider to be powerful in the various states and concentrates upon the most frequently mentioned reasons for this power. Naturally, the reasons for power will vary with the kind of group under consideration. Consider, for example, reasons given by legislators and lobbyists for the power of education and labor organizations (see Table 8.6).

As the table indicates, the major reason given for the perceived power of both groups is that they have large and potentially active memberships—memberships which can exercise power at the polls. However, there are basic differences to be observed in the secondary reasons given for the power of each group. For instance, economic power is rarely attributed to education groups but is mentioned occasionally as a reason for the power of labor organizations. The fact that education is a "sacred cow" is a substantial source of power for education lobbyists; but nobody considers labor to be a "sacred cow." Both legislators and lobbyists believe that education is of such importance that one can ill afford to neglect its needs; but nobody makes such a claim for organized labor. In the cases of both groups, however, the efforts of lobbyists rank as least important among the major reasons for the group's influence.

In order to pursue this last matter further, let us isolate those interest groups mentioned as powerful in only one state, such as the insurance lobby in Massachusetts, the trucking lobby in North Carolina, the business-associations lobby (Chamber of Commerce and Associated Industries of Oregon) in Oregon, and the mining lobby in Utah. As Table 8.7 indicates, in contrast to the large-membership organizations (education and labor), these interests (which are, in every case, business oriented) are accorded power because of their economic position within the state. Again, lobbying efforts rank relatively low as a source of power.

Thus, it appears that, while different groups receive their power from different sources, the efforts of lobbyists are never the major reason for power. There are, of course, substantial variations with regard to the perception of the extent to which lobbying efforts

TABLE 8.6

Reasons Offered for Power of Labor and Education Groups

	Massachusetts		North Carolina		Oregon		Utah	
	Legis-lators	Lobby-ists	Legis-lators	Lobby-ists	Legis-lators	Lobby-ists	Legis-lators	Lobby-ists
EDUCATION								
Large membership	42%	20%	44%	39%	37%	32%	32%	35%
Lobbying effort	15	13	21	21	27	15	39	29
"Sacred cow"	34	54	24	33	25	36	13	22
LABOR*								
Economic power	11	18			23	16	16	19
Large membership	67	62			58	62	41	55
Lobbying effort	14	16			12	14	38	25

* North Carolina excluded because of lack of labor lobbyists.

contribute to a group's power. It is clear, for instance, that lobbyists' efforts are considered substantially more important in Utah than they are in any of the other states (see Table 8.8). The perceived importance of lobby efforts in Utah might be a function of the fact that Utah legislators are so hostile to lobbyists yet accord them substantial influence.

TABLE 8.7

Reasons for Power of Selected Groups, by State

	Legislators	Lobbyists
INSURANCE: MASSACHUSETTS		
Economic power	41%	44%
Electoral strength	27	9
Lobbying effort	17	23
TRUCKING: NORTH CAROLINA		
Economic power	56	51
Electoral strength	14	12
Lobbying effort	24	29
BUSINESS ASSOCIATION: OREGON		
Economic power	31	40
Electoral strength	41	27
Lobbying effort	25	17
MINING: UTAH		
Economic power	41	58
Electoral strength	4	4
Lobbying effort	34	31

But, in spite of the variation in the case of Utah, the evidence does suggest that a group can achieve power *irrespective of the efforts of its lobbyists.* If a group has economic power or a large membership, it is likely to wield influence among legislators whatever its lobbyists do or do not do. However, the fact that the efforts of lobbyists do appear among the major reasons for the power of interest groups—even though these efforts are the least of those

TABLE 8.8

Percentage of Respondents Offering Lobbying
Efforts as Reason for Interest-Group Power

	Massachusetts	North Carolina	Oregon	Utah
Legislators	18%	21%	21%	38%
Lobbyists	20	30	20	31

major reasons—does suggest that lobby efforts can be useful in *maximizing* the potential power of an interest group. Groups powerful for the size of their memberships or for economic reasons will always be able to communicate with legislators, but it is probably true that a skilled lobbyist can lubricate the flow of communication. On the other hand, it is certainly not true that a group without outside resources can achieve success merely because it employs a skilled lobbyist. The skills of a lobbyist are without value unless the group has other resources.

9   CONCLUSIONS

Our use of interaction theory as the basis for an analysis of lobbying meant that we had to make some strategic decisions affecting the structure of the research. A fundamental commitment, once a suitable framework had been established, was to examine the perceptions of both legislators and lobbyists. This commitment had some rather obvious benefits—it enabled us, for instance, to view the interaction from the point of view of both participants—but also entailed some costs. In exploring a single set of relationships in depth, we were required to ignore, or at least minimize, a wider network of relationships established and maintained by legislators and lobbyists. Legislators interact with colleagues, constituents, party leaders, and administrators in addition to lobbyists. Rather than trying to describe the entire network of these interactions we "sliced away" a portion of the total network.

It is obviously true that one set of interactions is influenced by another. A legislator's view of his colleagues will affect his attitudes toward lobbyists, and his relationship with his party will influence his behavior with regard to interest groups. If a legislator is oriented toward receiving cues almost entirely from within the legislative chamber, "outsiders" such as lobbyists will have little influence on his thinking. However, a deliberate decision to explore one path of exchanges in depth does not necessarily result in a distorted picture of the "true" political life of legislators and lobbyists as long as the nature of the evidence is recognized and made explicit. For example, we describe lobbyists in Utah and Oregon as influential in comparison with lobbyists in Massachusetts and North Carolina. However, in comparison with other sources of influence within the state legislatures, lobbyists, even in Utah and Oregon, do not appear to be very effective. Thus, in the state with the strongest lobbies, Oregon, representatives of interest groups clearly do not dominate the decision-making process. They compete with other sources of information, albeit more successfully than do lobbyists in other states.

Just how it comes about that lobbyists are relatively successful in some states but not in others is a topic which this book has explored but certainly not resolved. The oft-stated assumption that political parties and interest groups compete for power, with one eventually "driving" the other out of the system, is a well-established canon of political science which is given some measure of support in this book. Massachusetts and North Carolina (both weak-lobby states) have stronger party organizations than do Oregon and Utah (strong-lobby states). However, economic and social variables, which are frequently used to explain both the output of legislatures and the behavior of political elites, do not seem to be consistently related to interest-group strength. Economically and socially, each pair of states has very little in common. However, Oregon and Utah are both "new" states, states with less-established political systems. To use a biological metaphor, their political systems are more "permeable," more open to the efforts of lobbyists.

We also found that the political game has higher economic stakes in Oregon and Utah than in Massachusetts and North Carolina. We suggest that higher stakes increase interaction between lobbyists and legislators. Increased interaction, in turn, enhances the probability of effective lobbying. States with high per-capita expenditures have more active lobbyists than states with low per-capita expenditures. Highly active lobbyists are able to establish relationships with legislators which can lead to persuasive communication.

The relationship between individual interaction and system-level variables could well stand further exploration. We found very little relationship between economic and social variables and interest-group strength. Yet we did note that the differing environments of the states do seem to contribute to variations as to which groups are represented by a larger number of lobbyists and which groups are perceived as most powerful. Thus, mining in Utah, lumber in Oregon, trucking in North Carolina, and insurance in Massachusetts are perceived as powerful groups and are well represented. In spite of the fact that labor (except in North Carolina) and education are the groups most frequently mentioned as powerful, there are clear state-by-state variations in their power which correspond roughly with the economic system of the state. However, it is not possible to base a theory of interest-group strength solely upon economic factors, because interaction with legislators is not limited to the economically dominant groups.

Granting the influence of some environmental variables, it is still true that interaction provides the most satisfying explanations of strengths and weaknesses in the lobbying process. Interaction between legislators and lobbyists is facilitated by overlap in their socioeconomic backgrounds, but is hindered by discrepancies in their career patterns and motivations. Legislators are self-starters and lobbyists are "drifters." In addition, legislators are politicized at an earlier age and are more ideologically motivated than are lobbyists. Thus, although both lobbyists and legislators are members of elites, beneath this superficial similarity lie two quite disparate career paths. Perhaps for this reason there is very little interchange between the two occupations. Nevertheless, a relationship (a stable pattern of interactions) can develop between a legislator and a lobbyist. The maintenance of such relationships enables lobbyists to achieve their goal of influencing the formation of public policy. Relationships between legislators and lobbyists develop because each has resources which the other needs. The relationship is not— at least initially—equal, since the legislator has the legal authority to cast a vote. In order to equalize the exchange, lobbyists must develop other resources—principally information. In order to become accepted as a legitimate source of information, lobbyists seek to establish a reputation for reliability. To gain such a reputation, a lobbyist must return to the legislature for several sessions and must become accepted as something more than a "one-shot" lobbyist.

Committed lobbyists—roughly 25 percent of those who register —are likely to identify both with their organizations and with their occupation. This dual identification strongly motivates them to spend a good deal of time with the legislature and to consider lobbying a relatively permanent career. Both of these factors are crucial in the establishment of effective communication.

How lobbyists develop a commitment to their job is a question which should be explored further. Lobbying, in spite of its relatively great financial reward, is a marginal occupation; the expectations attached to it are vague. Even lobbyists who consider themselves efficacious with regard to legislators feel themselves misunderstood by the "public." One might speculate that the glamor of the job (being in on important decisions) is attractive to certain kinds of individuals, individuals who enjoy a feeling of power. Yet, as we have seen, lobbying is much less spectacular than is commonly assumed. Lobbyists spend a substantial portion of their time in administrative work, rather than in actual contact work (although lobbyists in strong-lobby states spend more of their time in contact work than lobbyists in weak-lobby states).

Given the difficulties of the job, the turnover rate for lobbyists is surprisingly low; indeed, it is less than the rate for legislators. Those lobbyists who remain on the job can expect to increase their efficiency, because experienced legislators and lobbyists interact far more frequently than their less experienced counterparts, and interaction and positive attitude are closely related (although neither should be considered a "cause" of the other).

One of the most important consequences of sustained interaction is each participant's increased accuracy in estimating the attitudes of the other participant. The more frequently lobbyists and legislators interact, the more accurate become their evaluations of the other's feelings. Accuracy in estimating the feelings of the relevant other is particularly useful because it reduces the probability of error in behavior. Thus, the experienced lobbyist is an especially valuable agent. If the experienced lobbyist also has previous governmental experience, he is more valuable still.

Those lobbyists who have a firm commitment to an organization are those most likely to remain at the job long enough to become accepted as "veterans." However, commitment to an organization can weaken collegial relations with other lobbyists. In general, lobbyists have a difficult time developing occupational identification precisely because of their identification with an organization. However, the two identifications are not automatically in conflict, as is illustrated in the case of Oregon.

Whether or not a lobbyist is able to develop occupational identification, the perceptions of legislators give him a certain advantage. Legislators view lobbyists as more "professional" than they see themselves, and there is more consensus among legislators about the skills of lobbyists than about their own skills. This, however, is advantageous to the lobbyist only in certain states. In Oregon and

Utah, where amateurism is prized and professionalism is viewed with suspicion, lobbyists who appear too "polished" and adept can be at a disadvantage.

On the other hand, the participants' perceptions of the nature of the exchange between lobbyists and legislators always works to the advantage of the lobbyists. Legislators need information but resent pressure and do not like to think of themselves as vulnerable to the persuasive efforts of lobbyists. Consequently, they tend to view the exchange with lobbyists as informational rather than persuasive. Lobbyists, on the other hand, in keeping with their own self-image, view the exchange as persuasive. It does not matter which perception is accurate. As long as legislators *believe* they are receiving "neutral" information, the effectiveness of lobbyists is strengthened. If legislators were to agree with lobbyists' definition of the exchange (as persuasive), the effectiveness of lobbyists would be reduced. In this case, a congruence of perception would impair the efficiency of the communication. However, this exception proves the general rule that interaction leads to congruence of perception, which in turn leads to effective communication.

Effective communication can be interpreted—from the point of view of the lobbyist—as involving a satisfactory payoff in the form of the modification or reinforcement of the attitude of a legislator. The establishment of interaction is the key to success. Interpreting the effects of lobbying as a function of interaction ignores other variables—most obviously, it ignores the relationship between the personality of the legislator and his susceptibility to influence. However, though some legislators certainly are more vulnerable than others (primarily for psychological reasons unrelated to the resources and behavior of lobbyists), the factors contributing to vulnerability certainly are randomly distributed. When we consider the fact that a majority of legislators in Oregon and a substantial minority in the other states indicate impressive lobbyist influence, logic requires that we seek explanations more clearly related to the resources and perceptions surrounding the exchange situation.

Some of the conditions contributing to successful interaction, such as longevity and previous governmental experience, have already been dealt with. But we can add some other factors relating to the styles of the lobbyists. For instance, lobbyists should avoid being identified with "pressure tactics," since legislators who believe that they are a target for overtly persuasive communications are less likely to be influenced than those who perceive the communication to be neutral. The perception of a communication as benign is fostered by the existence of "rules of the game" governing lobbyist-legislator interaction. Such rules require that each actor follow—within certain broad areas—a "script," thus reducing the effect of any individual idiosyncracies in behavior.

Avoiding the appearance of pressure can be difficult for lobbyists representing groups viewed by most legislators as hostile. Perception of pressure is closely related to perception of ideological antagonism. Communications perceived as benign when they issue from a favored source may be perceived as threatening when they issue from a hostile source. The overriding importance of the source of the communication means that an interest group can exercise influence in the legislative process regardless of the activities of its lobbyists. Lobbyists can, of course, maximize the influence of their organizations by employing skillful techniques, and they can minimize influence by employing inept techniques. But lobbyists cannot create power. The greater the extralegislative resources of the interest group, the less important the job of the lobbyist. The influence of a particular lobbyist, thus, reflects the structure of power in a particular political system.

INDEX

205